LEARN XGBOOST

*Develop High-Performance Models
for Accurate Predictions*

Diego Rodrigues

LEARN XGBoost

Develop High-Performance Models for Accurate Predictions

2025 Edition

Author: Diego Rodrigues

studiod21portoalegre@gmail.com

Published by StudioD21.

Important Note

The codes and scripts presented in this book are primarily intended to illustrate, in a practical manner, the concepts discussed throughout the chapters. They were developed to demonstrate educational applications in controlled environments and may therefore require adaptations to function correctly in different contexts. It is the reader's responsibility to validate the specific configurations of their development environment before practical implementation.

More than providing ready-made solutions, this book seeks to encourage a solid understanding of the fundamentals covered, promoting critical thinking and technical autonomy. The examples presented should be seen as starting points for the reader to develop their own original solutions, adapted to the real demands of their career or projects. True technical competence arises from the ability to internalize essential principles and apply them creatively, strategically, and transformatively.

We therefore encourage each reader to go beyond mere reproduction of the examples, using this content as a foundation to build codes and scripts with their own identity, capable of generating a significant impact in their professional journey. This is the spirit of applied knowledge: to learn deeply to innovate with purpose.

We thank you for your trust and wish you a productive and inspiring learning journey.

CONTENTS

GREETINGS

Welcome to a carefully structured technical manual for the professional use of XGBoost, one of the most widely used algorithms for building high-performance supervised models. This content was developed with a focus on practical application, conceptual precision, and adherence to the requirements of real-world projects in business and operational environments.

In LEARN XGBoost – Develop High-Performance Models for Accurate Predictions, we present a modular, progressive, and results-oriented approach, following the principles of the TECHWRITE 2.3 Protocol. Each section has been organized to ensure didactic consistency, direct applicability, and clarity in technical decisions involving the use of XGBoost in different contexts — from data exploration to production deployment.

The goal of this material is to provide a solid foundation for building, evaluating, interpreting, and integrating predictive models based on XGBoost. Throughout the reading, concepts are presented objectively, scripts are explained in detail, and recommended practices are highlighted functionally, respecting the reality of those working with data in environments with concrete demands for performance and reliability.

This is a guide for professionals who need reproducible solutions, auditable techniques, and models that connect with strategic objectives. It is expected that the reading will effectively contribute to your work, offering clear tools for technical decision-making based on evidence, structure, and method.

Have a productive, structured, and technically transformative reading. You are on the right path.

ABOUT THE AUTHOR

Diego Rodrigues
Technical Author and Independent Researcher
ORCID: https://orcid.org/0009-0006-2178-634X
StudioD21 Smart Tech Content & Intell Systems
E-mail: studiod21portoalegre@gmail.com
LinkedIn: www.linkedin.com/in/diegoxpertai

International technical author (*tech writer*) focusing on structured production of applied knowledge. He is the founder of StudioD21 Smart Tech Content & Intell Systems, where he leads the creation of intelligent frameworks and the publication of technical textbooks supported by artificial intelligence, such as the Kali Linux Extreme series, SMARTBOOKS D21, among others.

Holder of 42 international certifications issued by institutions such as IBM, Google, Microsoft, AWS, Cisco, META, Ec-Council, Palo Alto and Boston University, he works in the fields of Artificial Intelligence, Machine Learning, Data Science, Big Data, Blockchain, Connectivity Technologies, Ethical Hacking and Threat Intelligence.

Since 2003, he has developed more than 200 technical projects for brands in Brazil, USA and Mexico. In 2024, he established himself as one of the greatest authors of technical books of the new generation, with more than 180 titles published in six languages. His work is based on his own applied technical writing protocol TECHWRITE 2.2, aimed at scalability, conceptual precision and practical applicability in professional

DIEGO RODRIGUES

environments.

BOOK PRESENTATION

Models based on structured data require technical precision, control over the pipeline, and a deep understanding of supervised learning mechanisms. XGBoost has established itself as one of the most effective libraries in this context, being widely adopted for its performance, stability, and adaptability to different operational scales. This book was conceived as a comprehensive technical manual, oriented toward the direct application of XGBoost in professional environments, with a rigorous modular structure and clear language, without loss of technical density.

The work begins with the theoretical foundations of the algorithm, its boosting-based architecture, and the operational differentials that justify its massive adoption in competitions, corporate projects, and production systems. Then, it addresses data preparation focusing on cleaning, encoding, and handling missing values, establishing a solid foundation for the supervised pipeline.

Model construction is covered in regression and binary classification, with emphasis on appropriate metrics, result interpretation, and fine-tuning of parameters. Techniques such as ROC curve analysis, threshold optimization, and the use of composite metrics ensure alignment between technical performance and business objectives.

Moving forward, the criteria for feature importance (gain, cover, frequency) and strategies for dimensionality reduction and model explainability are discussed. Overfitting control is explored through L1 and L2 regularizations, early stopping, and cross-validation.

Hyperparameter tuning with GridSearchCV and RandomizedSearchCV, evaluation with SHAP Values, multiclass modeling, and integration with structures like Pandas, NumPy, and time series expand the operational scope of the algorithm.

From an engineering standpoint, the content covers deployment with Flask and FastAPI, interactive interfaces with Streamlit, usage on GPU with CUDA support, and distributed execution with Dask, always focusing on reproducibility, security, and portability.

In business contexts, issues such as versioning, cross-team validation, production checkpoints, model governance, and integration with legacy systems are addressed. The final checklist consolidates the stability and delivery criteria required in critical environments.

Each topic was crafted to reflect the real demands of projects involving data, predictive logic, and application integration. The progression favors both continuous study and use as a technical reference material. The book is not intended to be introductory, but functional, consistent, and ready for what XGBoost offers most relevantly: accurate prediction, with control and depth.

Here, theory becomes practice — and practice
becomes technical mastery.

CHAPTER 1. INTRODUCTION TO XGBOOST

XGBoost, short for eXtreme Gradient Boosting, has established itself as one of the most powerful and efficient libraries for supervised learning tasks, especially in data science competitions, business applications, and projects with critical performance requirements. This chapter introduces the essential fundamentals of the technique, focusing on understanding the motivation, internal architecture, strengths, and differentiators of XGBoost compared to other machine learning approaches.

Direct Application of the Topic

The objective of this chapter is to provide a functional view of XGBoost: what it is, why it performs so well, in which scenarios it is preferred, and how its internal structure makes it one of the most widely used frameworks for classification, regression, and ranking tasks.

XGBoost is not just a Boosting library — it represents a highly optimized implementation of the Gradient Boosting algorithm, with significant advancements in computational performance, regularization, parallelization, and scalability.

Without focusing on historical background or curiosities, the focus here is to understand why XGBoost is technically superior to traditional libraries such as sklearn.ensemble.GradientBoostingClassifier, AdaBoost, or Random Forests in various production scenarios.

Basic Execution with Code

A minimal execution of XGBoost in Python can be performed with just a few commands:

python

```
from xgboost import XGBClassifier
from sklearn.datasets import load_breast_cancer
from sklearn.model_selection import train_test_split


# Data loading
X, y = load_breast_cancer(return_X_y=True)


# Train-test split
X_train, X_test, y_train, y_test = train_test_split(X, y,
test_size=0.3)


# Instantiation and training
model = XGBClassifier()
model.fit(X_train, y_train)
```

This example encapsulates the essence of XGBoost: a simple API, compatible with scikit-learn, but with extremely robust internal capabilities.

Functional Variations

XGBoost can be used not only for binary classification, as shown in the previous example, but also for regression (XGBRegressor), multiclass classification (objective='multi:softmax'), and ranking problems (with XGBRanker).

Moreover, the library allows different modes of data input:

NumPy arrays, Pandas DataFrames, or optimized objects called DMatrix, which store metadata such as weights, labels, and missing values more efficiently.

Below, an example using DMatrix:

python

```
import xgboost as xgb


dtrain = xgb.DMatrix(X_train, label=y_train)
dtest = xgb.DMatrix(X_test)


params = {
    'max_depth': 3,
    'eta': 0.1,
    'objective': 'binary:logistic'
}


bst = xgb.train(params, dtrain, num_boost_round=10)
```

This method offers advanced control over the boosting process, being preferred in high-performance applications.

System Behavior

During training, XGBoost builds decision trees sequentially, where each new tree tries to correct the errors made by the previous ones. The final model is composed of the weighted sum of all trees.

The internal behavior is governed by:

- Information gain: criteria based on error reduction (gain) to select splits.

- Regularization: penalizes trees that are too deep or with too many leaves.

- Shrinkage (or learning rate): controls the contribution of each tree.

- Subsampling: introduces randomness to avoid overfitting.

- This mechanism results in more accurate models and less prone to overfitting compared to purely bagging-based approaches like Random Forests.

Control and Monitoring

XGBoost provides several features to control the learning process:

- eval_metric: defines evaluation metrics during training.
- early_stopping_rounds: automatically stops training if there is no improvement after N iterations.
- evals: allows passing validation sets for continuous monitoring.

Example with early stopping:

python

```
evals = [(dtrain, 'train'), (dtest, 'eval')]


bst = xgb.train(params, dtrain, num_boost_round=100,
evals=evals, early_stopping_rounds=10)
```

Training is interrupted if the evaluation metric on the eval set does not improve after 10 consecutive rounds, saving computational time and preventing overfitting.

Technical Differentials of XGBoost

XGBoost's architecture stands out for offering:

- Regularized Boosting: combination of L1 and L2 for complexity control.

- Block structure for splits: accelerates the search for the best splits.

- Sparsity support: natively handles missing values and sparse datasets.

- Internal parallelization: uses multiple cores by default to build trees.

- GPU support: possibility to significantly accelerate training with CUDA.

- Custom objectives: allows definition of custom loss functions.

These aspects make XGBoost especially useful in production environments where performance, fine control, and reliability are essential.

Comparison with Other Libraries

Library	Regularization	GPU	Early Stopping	Custom Objective	Speed
XGBoost	Yes	Yes	Yes	Yes	High
scikit-learn GBC	No	No	Yes (manual)	No	Medium
LightGBM	Yes	Yes	Yes	Yes	High
CatBoost	Yes	Yes	Yes	Yes	High
Random Forest	No	No	No	No	Medium

Although LightGBM and CatBoost are modern alternatives, XGBoost maintains a solid foundation due to its balance between robustness, documentation, and compatibility with diverse ecosystems.

Common Use Cases

- Binary churn classification
- Credit scoring
- Demand forecasting
- Medical diagnosis based on exams
- Fraud detection
- Pattern recognition in transactional data

Its flexibility and high performance make it applicable to any supervised problem where accuracy and interpretability are key factors.

Final Considerations

This chapter laid out the main technical and functional concepts of XGBoost. Understanding its structure and internal behavior is essential to fully leverage the library in the following chapters, which will cover:

- Hyperparameter optimization
- Feature importance analysis
- Integration with deployment and monitoring tools
- Advanced cases with GPU, Dask, SageMaker, and more

XGBoost is not just a library — it is a solid foundation for professionals who want to deliver high-precision predictions with absolute control over the machine learning pipeline.

CHAPTER 2. DATA PREPARATION FOR XGBOOST

The performance of any machine learning model is directly linked to the quality of the data used in its training. In the case of XGBoost, this relationship is even more sensitive because its structure based on successive decision trees amplifies patterns, outliers, and inconsistencies present in the dataset. This chapter presents, in a practical and structured way, how to effectively prepare data to maximize the performance of models built with XGBoost. The steps involve data analysis and cleaning, categorical variable encoding, and handling of missing values, all executed with a focus on model stability, robustness, and predictive capability.

Basic Execution with Code

Data preparation begins with exploratory analysis and consistency checking. Suppose a sales dataset with categorical columns, null values, and different data types:

python

```
import pandas as pd


df = pd.read_csv('vendas.csv')
print(df.dtypes)
print(df.isnull().sum())
print(df.describe(include='all'))
```

After this preliminary analysis, the first task is basic data cleaning, removing irrelevant columns, duplicate values, and clearly inconsistent entries:

python

```
df.drop(columns=['ID', 'DataRegistro'], inplace=True)

df.drop_duplicates(inplace=True)

df = df[df['ValorVenda'] > 0]
```

Next, we handle categorical variables and missing values, preparing the dataset for use with XGBoost.

Functional Variations

There are multiple ways to handle categorical variables. XGBoost requires numerical input, so it is necessary to encode any categorical column. The two main approaches are:

One-Hot Encoding, ideal for variables with low cardinality:

python

```
df = pd.get_dummies(df, columns=['Produto', 'Região'])
```

Label Encoding, more memory-efficient but sensitive to implicit ordering:

python

```
from sklearn.preprocessing import LabelEncoder


le = LabelEncoder()

df['Produto'] = le.fit_transform(df['Produto'])
```

```
df['Região'] = le.fit_transform(df['Região'])
```

The choice depends on the volume of categories, dataset size, and whether XGBClassifier or XGBRegressor will be used.

For missing values, strategies vary according to the type of data:

Filling with mean, median, or mode:

python

```
df['Idade'].fillna(df['Idade'].median(), inplace=True)
```

Filling with a fixed value or "unknown" category:

python

```
df['Categoria'].fillna('Indefinido', inplace=True)
```

Exclusion of incomplete records in extreme cases:

python

```
df.dropna(inplace=True)
```

System Behavior

During training, XGBoost interprets null values differently. When using DMatrix, the library automatically identifies missing values and learns during the splitting process how to handle them in the best way. This can even generate specific splits for missing values, improving performance in some contexts.

python

```
import xgboost as xgb
```

```python
X = df.drop(columns='Alvo')
y = df['Alvo']
dtrain = xgb.DMatrix(X, label=y, missing=np.nan)
```

Using missing=np.nan ensures that XGBoost handles nulls optimally. The default behavior avoids the need for manual imputation, but this depends on the consistency of the rest of the pipeline.

Control and Monitoring

Data preparation needs to be verifiable and reproducible. For this, it is recommended to:

Check descriptive statistics after cleaning:

python

```python
print(df.describe())
```

Check if there are any non-numeric columns not yet converted:

python

```python
print(df.select_dtypes(include='object').columns)
```

Validate if the number of samples after cleaning matches the original volume:

python

```python
print(f"Lines after cleaning: {len(df)}")
```

Use tools like Sweetviz, Pandas Profiling, or YData Profiling for automated auditing:

python

```
import ydata_profiling

profile = ydata_profiling.ProfileReport(df)
profile.to_file("relatorio.html")
```

This type of auditing is essential in corporate environments or pipelines with multiple stakeholders, avoiding reprocessing and later conflicts.

Common Error Resolution

Error: ValueError: could not convert string to float
Cause: Categorical column not converted.
Solution: Apply appropriate encoding before passing to XGBoost.

Error: Data contains NaN values
Cause: Data with unidentified missing values.
Solution: Use the missing=np.nan parameter or impute the data.

Error: Mismatch in feature number between training and prediction
Cause: One-hot encoding with different categories between training and test.
Solution: Ensure consistency using ColumnTransformer or manually fix columns.

Error: Columns with high cardinality causing memory overflow
Cause: Application of One-Hot to columns with too many categories.
Solution: Replace with Label Encoding or group rare categories.

Error: Model not improving despite high-quality data

Cause: Presence of noisy variables or multicollinearity.

Solution: Apply correlation analysis and remove redundant variables.

Best Practices

- Apply dropna() with criteria based on impact and not indiscriminately

- Use LabelEncoder only when there is no risk of order inference

- Consolidate rare categories to avoid excessive sparsity

- Create reproducible scripts with logging of preprocessing steps

- Validate encoding and imputation after each transformation with .info() and .head()

Strategic Summary

Data preparation is a critical step for the success of models based on XGBoost. The quality of the data fed into the library determines not only the final accuracy but also the training time, risk of overfitting, and pipeline stability. With proper cleaning, encoding, and handling of missing values, it is possible to ensure a more robust and reliable modeling environment.

The steps carried out in this chapter — from initial analysis to final encoding — represent the foundation upon which models will be built. They also enable smooth application of cross-validation, hyperparameter tuning, and production deployment. Every decision made at this stage directly impacts the next phases.

CHAPTER 3. FUNDAMENTAL CONCEPTS OF BOOSTING

Understanding XGBoost requires a clear comprehension of the concepts that underpin the Boosting algorithm. Unlike other approaches such as Bagging, Boosting is based on sequential learning, in which each new model is trained to correct the errors made by the previous ones. This successive refinement, combined with weighting and regularization strategies, is what gives XGBoost its reputation for high performance. This chapter presents the differences between Bagging and Boosting, the internal workings of Gradient Boosting, and the technical differentiators that make XGBoost superior in various supervised learning scenarios.

The main difference between Bagging and Boosting lies in the training strategy. While Bagging builds multiple independent models on random subsets of the dataset (as in Random Forest), Boosting builds models sequentially, where each new model tries to improve the ensemble's performance by focusing on the errors of the previous model. This process leads to the formation of a committee of weak models that, when combined, become extremely powerful.

To understand the impact of this difference, consider that in Bagging the final model is an average or a vote of all parallel models' results. In Boosting, the final model is a weighted sum of successive predictors, each adjusted to minimize the remaining errors of the previous ones. In XGBoost, this adjustment is done with a gradient-based approach, providing greater control and faster convergence.

Gradient Boosting, which serves as the foundation for XGBoost, uses a technique called "functional gradient descent." Instead of directly adjusting predicted values, the algorithm adjusts the residuals — that is, the difference between the true value and the predicted value — trying to minimize them gradually with each new tree.

At each iteration, the algorithm builds a new decision tree that tries to predict these residuals. This tree is then added to the model with a learning rate that reduces the impact of the new tree to avoid overfitting. The sequence is repeated until a defined number of trees is built or the validation error stops decreasing.

A cycle of the algorithm involves:

- Calculation of the loss based on the current predictions

- Calculation of the gradient of the loss function

- Training of a new tree to predict this gradient

- Updating the predictions based on the results of the new tree

This process occurs in short cycles but in an extremely effective way, resulting in models with high predictive capability.

XGBoost takes this logic to a new level by incorporating several structural optimizations. Among the main differentiators are:

- Explicit regularization with L1 (Lasso) and L2 (Ridge) penalties

- Native support for missing values

- Parallelization support in tree training

- Memory optimization with block structures for columns

- Tree growth based on maximum depth instead of number of leaves

- Full support for early stopping, checkpoints, and custom metrics

These improvements enable XGBoost to deliver highly accurate models, robust to noise, and adaptable to a wide variety of problems.

Below, the basic operation of Gradient Boosting can be observed with a simplified code using scikit-learn, which shares the same conceptual basis:

python

```python
from sklearn.ensemble import GradientBoostingClassifier

from sklearn.datasets import make_classification

from sklearn.model_selection import train_test_split

from sklearn.metrics import accuracy_score


X, y = make_classification(n_samples=1000, n_features=20, random_state=42)

X_train, X_test, y_train, y_test = train_test_split(X, y, test_size=0.2)


model = GradientBoostingClassifier(n_estimators=100, learning_rate=0.1, max_depth=3)

model.fit(X_train, y_train)

y_pred = model.predict(X_test)
```

```
print("Accuracy:", accuracy_score(y_test, y_pred))
```

In XGBoost, the same procedure can be done with more efficiency, control, and better memory management:

python

```
from xgboost import XGBClassifier
```

```
model = XGBClassifier(n_estimators=100, learning_rate=0.1,
max_depth=3, use_label_encoder=False, eval_metric='logloss')
model.fit(X_train, y_train)
y_pred = model.predict(X_test)
```

```
print("Accuracy:", accuracy_score(y_test, y_pred))
```

The advantage of XGBoost starts to stand out in larger datasets, with complex categorical columns, the presence of missing values, and the need for detailed parameter control.

In addition, XGBoost offers additional metrics, such as AUC, logloss, error, merror, and the ability to monitor training progress with multiple validation sets:

python

```
eval_set = [(X_train, y_train), (X_test, y_test)]
model.fit(X_train, y_train, eval_set=eval_set,
early_stopping_rounds=10, verbose=True)
```

This type of mechanism is essential in business environments with multiple testing and production cycles.

Unlike Bagging, which does not prioritize more difficult cases, Boosting concentrates its efforts on improving the points where previous models failed. This allows for more refined learning, but also becomes more susceptible to overfitting if not properly controlled with regularization, cross-validation, and careful use of parameters like learning_rate and max_depth.

Among the most important parameters of XGBoost are:

- n_estimators: number of trees to be built

- learning_rate: learning rate that regulates the impact of each tree

- max_depth: maximum depth of the trees

- subsample: percentage of samples used per tree

- colsample_bytree: percentage of columns used per tree

- reg_alpha and reg_lambda: L1 and L2 regularization controls

These parameters are critical for controlling model bias and variance and should be carefully adjusted according to the problem and data volume.

The sequential structure of Boosting has direct implications on execution in parallel environments. While Bagging can be easily parallelized, Boosting requires that each step waits for the completion of the previous one. To mitigate this, XGBoost implements parallelization in the construction of splits within each tree, using multiple cores to simultaneously find the best split points.

Additionally, the use of the DMatrix format further optimizes the process by preprocessing the data into high-performance binary structures:

python

```python
import xgboost as xgb

dtrain = xgb.DMatrix(X_train, label=y_train)
dtest = xgb.DMatrix(X_test, label=y_test)

params = {
    'max_depth': 3,
    'eta': 0.1,
    'objective': 'binary:logistic',
    'eval_metric': 'logloss'
}

model = xgb.train(params, dtrain, num_boost_round=100,
evals=[(dtest, 'eval')])
```

With this level of control, it is possible to integrate XGBoost into sophisticated pipelines with experiment tracking, model versioning, deployment via APIs, and real-time monitoring.

Understanding the concepts of Boosting, its differences from Bagging, and the particularities of Gradient Boosting are fundamental to applying XGBoost strategically, extracting maximum performance with minimal risk of overfitting or underutilization of the data.

Common Error Resolution

Error: ValueError: feature names mismatch
Cause: Training and prediction with columns in different orders.
Solution: Ensure consistency in preprocessing and save feature names with the model.

Error: Overfitting with high training accuracy but low test accuracy
Cause: Trees too deep or learning rate too high.
Solution: Reduce max_depth, apply early_stopping_rounds, or decrease eta.

Error: Slow training with large volumes of data
Cause: Using standard structures instead of DMatrix.
Solution: Use xgb.DMatrix() and configure parallelization correctly.

Error: RuntimeError: GPU device not found
Cause: tree_method='gpu_hist' parameter activated on a machine without CUDA support.
Solution: Check compatibility or use tree_method='hist'.

Error: ImportError when trying to run the model in production
Cause: Version differences between development and production environments.
Solution: Use virtualenvs and save environments with pip freeze.

Best Practices

- Adjust learning_rate to smaller values and increase n_estimators for refined gains

- Monitor multiple metrics simultaneously with the eval_metric parameter

- Use cross-validation (cross_val_score) whenever possible for greater robustness

- Avoid using One-Hot Encoding on columns with high cardinality

- Apply regularization even on small datasets for greater stability

Strategic Summary

The concepts of Boosting form the core of the understanding needed to master XGBoost. Understanding the fundamental difference from Bagging, the operation of Gradient Boosting, and the optimizations incorporated into XGBoost allows you to apply the library with much greater confidence and control. Mastery of these theoretical foundations, aligned with the practical use of parameters and control techniques, defines the maturity of the data scientist or engineer seeking high performance in real-world projects. Moving forward, this knowledge will enable more accurate results, with lower computational cost and greater alignment with business objectives.

CHAPTER 4. INSTALLATION AND ENVIRONMENT CONFIGURATION

The correct installation of XGBoost and the proper configuration of the working environment are essential prerequisites for the development of any pipeline with the library. Compatibility issues, missing dependencies, and inconsistencies in virtual environments can compromise the entire experimentation and production flow. This chapter presents the installation process via pip and conda, the creation of isolated environments to ensure reproducibility, and the fundamental tests to validate whether the setup is ready for the technical use of XGBoost with high performance.

The simplest and most direct way to install XGBoost is through pip, the standard package manager for Python. In systems with an updated Python version and modern compilers, the standard installation is usually sufficient:

bash

```
pip install xgboost
```

In some cases, it may be necessary to update pip to ensure that the latest version of the package is accessible:

bash

```
python -m pip install --upgrade pip
```

After installation, it is recommended to check the installed version with the following command:

python

```
import xgboost
print(xgboost.__version__)
```

Another widely used approach in data science environments is installation via conda, which automatically handles native library dependencies and C++ compilation:

bash

```
conda install -c conda-forge xgboost
```

The advantage of conda is that it handles GPU environments and complex dependencies such as libgomp, which are necessary for XGBoost's internal functioning in Linux environments.

To ensure that different projects do not conflict due to different library versions, it is highly recommended to create isolated environments using venv or conda. Below, an example of environment creation with venv:

bash

```
python -m venv xgb_env
source xgb_env/bin/activate # Linux/Mac
xgb_env\Scripts\activate.bat # Windows
pip install xgboost
```

With the environment activated, all libraries installed will be isolated within that project, preventing interference with other existing Python environments on the machine.

Additionally, it is recommended to install auxiliary libraries for environment validation:

bash

```bash
pip install pandas scikit-learn matplotlib
```

With the libraries installed, the next step is to validate if XGBoost is operating correctly. Below, a minimal code to test model functionality:

python

```python
from xgboost import XGBClassifier
from sklearn.datasets import load_iris


X, y = load_iris(return_X_y=True)
model = XGBClassifier(use_label_encoder=False,
eval_metric='mlogloss')
model.fit(X, y)
```

This test ensures that the installation is functional and that dependencies such as numpy, scikit-learn, and compilers were correctly recognized by the system.

For environments with GPU support, XGBoost can be compiled with CUDA support. However, the standard installation via pip does not include binaries for GPU execution. In these cases, it is ideal to use conda:

bash

```bash
conda install -c nvidia -c rapidsai -c conda-forge \
    xgboost=1.7.3 \
    python=3.9 \
```

```
cudatoolkit=11.2
```

This command ensures that the correct version of the library is aligned with the machine's CUDA driver version. After that, simply configure the tree_method as gpu_hist when instantiating the model:

python

```python
model = XGBClassifier(tree_method='gpu_hist')
```

Another important point is the use of libraries to check the available environment and hardware:

python

```python
import os
import platform

print("System:", platform.system())
print("CUDA available:", 'NVIDIA System Management Interface' in os.popen("nvidia-smi").read())
```

This initial check prevents setups from being executed in environments without proper support, saving time and avoiding silent failures.

For teams sharing the environment, it is fundamental to generate requirement files that guarantee reproducibility of the installation:

bash

```bash
pip freeze > requirements.txt
```

Or, in conda environments:

bash

conda env export > environment.yml

These files can be used to recreate the environment on another machine identically.

In more advanced pipelines, the recommended practice is to encapsulate the environment within containers using Docker. A minimal Dockerfile for XGBoost might contain:

dockerfile

```
FROM python:3.9
RUN pip install xgboost scikit-learn pandas
```

Thus, the environment becomes portable, scalable, and less prone to failures due to version divergences.

Correct environment configuration is therefore a strategic step that ensures not only the proper functioning of XGBoost but also the scalability and consistency of the projects that use it.

Common Error Resolution

Error: ImportError: libgomp.so.1: cannot open shared object file
Cause: Missing dependency in Linux systems.
Solution: Install the libgomp1 package via apt or use conda.

Error: OSError: [WinError 126] The specified module could not be found
Cause: Lack of binary compatibility on Windows.
Solution: Install via conda, which automatically resolves native

dependencies.

Error: ModuleNotFoundError: No module named 'xgboost'
Cause: Library not installed or virtual environment not activated.
Solution: Check if the environment is active and install with pip install xgboost.

Error: ValueError: Invalid tree_method: gpu_hist
Cause: Parameter activated on a machine without GPU or CUDA support.
Solution: Replace with tree_method='hist' or install XGBoost with CUDA support.

Error: RuntimeError when trying to import XGBoost in notebooks
Cause: Jupyter environment different from terminal environment.
Solution: Ensure the Jupyter kernel is using the same Python from the virtual environment.

Best Practices

- Use isolated virtual environments with venv or conda for each project

- Check the library and Python versions immediately after installation

- Install auxiliary libraries like scikit-learn, pandas, and matplotlib for testing and validation
- Use requirements.txt or environment.yml files to ensure reproducibility

- Check GPU compatibility before configuring tree_method='gpu_hist'

Strategic Summary

The correct installation of XGBoost and environment configuration form the foundation for any consistent technical project with machine learning. Ensuring that all dependencies are installed, that the environment is isolated, and that initial tests run without error is the most efficient way to avoid problems in later pipeline phases. Mastery of this process reduces debugging time, improves team collaboration, and increases the reliability of results. By aligning your development environment with the library's requirements, you turn XGBoost into a powerful ally for high-performance deliveries.

CHAPTER 5. TRAINING WITH XGBOOST REGRESSOR

The use of XGBoost for regression tasks enables the construction of robust and high-performance models capable of predicting continuous values with precision. This type of application is widely used in contexts such as price forecasting, demand prediction, energy consumption, risk assessment, and other scenarios where the target variable is not categorical but numerical. This chapter demonstrates the basic execution of a regression model with XGBoost, including evaluation by appropriate metrics and the correct interpretation of results for practical application.

The first step consists of loading the data and preparing the training set. For exemplification, the California housing price dataset from the sklearn library will be used, which contains multiple numerical variables:

python

```python
from sklearn.datasets import fetch_california_housing

from sklearn.model_selection import train_test_split

from xgboost import XGBRegressor


# Data loading
data = fetch_california_housing()
X = data.data
```

```
y = data.target
```

```
# Train-test split
X_train, X_test, y_train, y_test = train_test_split(X, y,
test_size=0.2, random_state=42)
```

With the data ready, the execution of the XGBRegressor model can be done with just a few commands. Below is the minimum code necessary to train and predict with the model:

python

```
model = XGBRegressor(n_estimators=100, learning_rate=0.1,
max_depth=3)

model.fit(X_train, y_train)

y_pred = model.predict(X_test)
```

This model is already functional and delivers quite competitive initial results. Next, it is necessary to evaluate its performance with appropriate metrics for regression.

The most recommended evaluation metrics in regression tasks are:

- MSE (Mean Squared Error): heavily penalizes large errors

- RMSE (Root Mean Squared Error): error value on the same scale as the target

- MAE (Mean Absolute Error): mean of absolute errors, less sensitive to outliers

- R^2 Score: percentage of variability explained by the model

Below, an example of how to calculate these metrics with sklearn:

python

```
from sklearn.metrics import mean_squared_error,
mean_absolute_error, r2_score

import numpy as np


mse = mean_squared_error(y_test, y_pred)

rmse = np.sqrt(mse)

mae = mean_absolute_error(y_test, y_pred)

r2 = r2_score(y_test, y_pred)


print("MSE:", mse)

print("RMSE:", rmse)

print("MAE:", mae)

print("R²:", r2)
```

These metrics provide a clear view of the model's accuracy. RMSE and MAE, for example, are especially useful when the objective is to understand the average error in real units (such as dollars or square meters).

The interpretation of the results should consider the mean absolute deviation (MAE) and mean squared error (MSE) in relation to the scale of the target variable. An RMSE much larger than the target mean indicates instability or the need for adjustment. An R^2 close to 1 indicates that the model is explaining the data variability well. Negative R^2 indicates a model worse than simply predicting the mean.

In addition to metric values, it is important to visualize the error distribution to identify bias patterns. A scatter plot between predicted and actual values can reveal if the model tends to underestimate or overestimate in certain target ranges:

python

```
import matplotlib.pyplot as plt


plt.scatter(y_test, y_pred, alpha=0.3)

plt.xlabel("Actual values")

plt.ylabel("Predictions")

plt.title("Actual vs Predicted")

plt.show()
```

This type of visualization helps detect structural failures such as heteroscedasticity (increasing error variance), common in financial and market datasets.

Another point of attention is the model's behavior during the training process. It is possible to monitor the error in real-time with eval_set and early_stopping_rounds, which stops training if the model does not show improvement:

python

```
eval_set = [(X_train, y_train), (X_test, y_test)]

model = XGBRegressor(n_estimators=1000,
learning_rate=0.05)

model.fit(X_train, y_train, early_stopping_rounds=20,
eval_set=eval_set, verbose=True)
```

This not only saves training time but also prevents overfitting. When the validation set error starts to rise while the training set error keeps dropping, the model is overfitting the training patterns and generalizing poorly to new data.

Regression with XGBoost allows fine-tuning through hyperparameters such as:

- n_estimators: number of trees

- learning_rate: defines the size of correction steps

- max_depth: maximum depth of trees

- subsample: proportion of rows used per tree

- colsample_bytree: proportion of columns used per tree

- gamma: penalization for splits with small gain

- reg_alpha and reg_lambda: L1 and L2 regularization controls

These parameters must be adjusted based on experiments and cross-validation, using GridSearchCV or RandomizedSearchCV, approaches that will be explored in later chapters.

It is also possible to save and reload the trained model for later use, using joblib:

python

```
import joblib
joblib.dump(model, 'modelo_xgb.pkl')
modelo_carregado = joblib.load('modelo_xgb.pkl')
```

This is essential in real pipelines where the model will be used in multiple moments and environments, including production.

Building regression models with XGBoost requires not only good hyperparameter tuning but also a critical analysis of evaluation metrics and model behavior. The use of auxiliary visualizations, cross-validation, and early stopping are fundamental strategies to ensure robustness.

Common Error Resolution

Error: ValueError: could not convert string to float
Cause: Categorical data not encoded before training.
Solution: Apply Label Encoding or One-Hot Encoding to categorical columns.

Error: Model performance very low (negative R^2)
Cause: Poorly distributed target variable or no clear relation with features.
Solution: Reevaluate feature engineering, normalize data, and test new derived attributes.

Error: Model with RMSE much larger than the target mean
Cause: Extreme outliers affecting the quadratic error.
Solution: Apply outlier treatment or use MAE as the main metric.

Error: The model stopped improving even after increasing the number of trees
Cause: High learning rate or early overfitting.
Solution: Reduce learning_rate, apply early_stopping_rounds, and increase n_estimators.

Error: Cannot cast array data from dtype('O') to dtype('float64')
Cause: Presence of non-numeric objects or strings in dataset columns.

Solution: Check types with df.dtypes and correctly convert before training.

Best Practices

- Use XGBRegressor with early_stopping_rounds to avoid overfitting

- Evaluate the model with multiple metrics: RMSE, MAE, and R^2

- Visualize errors with scatter plots between actual and predicted values

- Adjust learning_rate to low values and gradually increase n_estimators

- Monitor error curves with eval_set to understand model behavior

Strategic Summary

Training with XGBRegressor represents one of the most direct and powerful applications of XGBoost for problems with numerical target variables. With a few commands, it is possible to train models that outperform linear regressions and even neural networks in several contexts. The key to success lies in the alignment between well-prepared data, adjusted hyperparameters, and continuous performance evaluation. This solid regression foundation will support more advanced integrations with production pipelines, multivariate analyses, and time series applications.

CHAPTER 6. CLASSIFICATION WITH XGBOOST CLASSIFIER

Binary classification is one of the most frequent applications of XGBoost in machine learning projects. Identifying whether a customer will cancel a service, whether a transaction is fraudulent, or whether an email is spam or legitimate are examples of binary tasks that require precise, scalable, and interpretable models. The XGBoost Classifier offers advanced features for this type of problem, including support for custom metrics, fine-tuning of decision thresholds, and visualization of the ROC curve with AUC. This chapter presents the construction of a binary classification model with XGBoost, evaluation based on probability, and control of the decision cutoff point.

The initial structure of a binary classification problem with XGBoost follows the same basic pattern of data preparation. Assuming a dataset with labels 0 and 1, the separation between predictor variables and the target variable begins:

python

```
from sklearn.model_selection import train_test_split

from sklearn.datasets import load_breast_cancer

from xgboost import XGBClassifier


# Data loading

data = load_breast_cancer()

X = data.data
```

```python
y = data.target
```

```python
# Train-test split
X_train, X_test, y_train, y_test = train_test_split(X, y,
test_size=0.3, random_state=42)
```

With the data separated, creating the model is straightforward and highly configurable. Below, a model with minimum parameters, ready for a first round of training:

python

```python
model = XGBClassifier(use_label_encoder=False,
eval_metric='logloss')
model.fit(X_train, y_train)
```

The evaluation of binary classification with XGBoost must always consider the probabilistic nature of the output. By default, the .predict() method returns classes 0 or 1, based on the default threshold of 0.5. For a more detailed analysis, using .predict_proba() allows visualization of the probability of the positive class for each observation:

python

```python
y_proba = model.predict_proba(X_test)[:, 1]
```

From this probability, the model's cutoff point can be adjusted according to the context of the problem. In scenarios with strong class imbalance or different costs for false positives and false negatives, the threshold can be manually calibrated:

python

```python
import numpy as np


threshold = 0.3
y_pred_adjusted = (y_proba >= threshold).astype(int)
```

Choosing a threshold lower than 0.5 increases sensitivity (recall) at the expense of precision. This calibration is especially useful in areas like healthcare, finance, and security, where underestimating is costlier than overestimating.

Visualization of the ROC curve (Receiver Operating Characteristic) and the calculation of the area under this curve (AUC – Area Under the Curve) are standard tools for evaluating the model's overall performance:

python

```python
from sklearn.metrics import roc_curve, auc
import matplotlib.pyplot as plt


fpr, tpr, _ = roc_curve(y_test, y_proba)
roc_auc = auc(fpr, tpr)


plt.plot(fpr, tpr, label=f'ROC Curve (AUC = {roc_auc:.2f})')
plt.plot([0, 1], [0, 1], linestyle='--', color='gray')
plt.xlabel('False Positive')
plt.ylabel('True Positive')
plt.title('ROC Curve')
plt.legend()
```

```
plt.show()
```

The closer the ROC curve is to the upper left corner, the better the model's performance. AUC values close to 1 indicate excellent class separation.

In addition to the ROC curve, other useful metrics include:

- Precision: proportion of correct positive predictions

- Recall: proportion of actual positives identified
- F1 Score: harmonic mean between precision and recall

- Confusion Matrix: complete visualization of hits and errors

These metrics can be easily extracted with sklearn:

python

```python
from sklearn.metrics import classification_report,
confusion_matrix


print(classification_report(y_test, y_pred_adjusted))
print(confusion_matrix(y_test, y_pred_adjusted))
```

For projects with imbalanced data, using scale_pos_weight can improve performance. This parameter adjusts the weight of the minority class during training:

python

```python
model = XGBClassifier(use_label_encoder=False,
eval_metric='logloss', scale_pos_weight=2)
```

```python
model.fit(X_train, y_train)
```

The ideal value for scale_pos_weight should consider the ratio between the number of negative and positive instances. This improves sensitivity without drastically increasing false positives.

It is also possible to use early_stopping_rounds to automatically stop training upon detecting overfitting:

python

```python
eval_set = [(X_test, y_test)]

model.fit(X_train, y_train, eval_set=eval_set,
early_stopping_rounds=10, verbose=True)
```

This mechanism allows XGBoost to stop when validation error ceases to improve, avoiding excessive iterations and computational resource waste.

In more controlled environments, it is recommended to use cross-validation to evaluate model stability. This can be done with cross_val_score or StratifiedKFold to maintain the class proportion:

python

```python
from sklearn.model_selection import StratifiedKFold,
cross_val_score


kfold = StratifiedKFold(n_splits=5, shuffle=True,
random_state=42)

scores = cross_val_score(model, X, y, cv=kfold,
scoring='roc_auc')

print("Average AUC:", np.mean(scores))
```

This type of validation provides a more robust view of overall performance, avoiding misleading interpretations based on a single data partition.

The XGBoost Classifier also offers resources to interpret the model through feature importance. The attribute feature_importances_ shows the relative contribution of each feature to the final decision:

python

```
importances = model.feature_importances_
for name, importance in zip(data.feature_names, importances):
    print(f'{name}: {importance:.4f}')
```

Analyzing these importances can serve as a guide to refine the model, eliminate redundant variables, and better understand system behavior.

Common Error Resolution

Error: ValueError: y contains previously unseen labels
Cause: Output column with different values between training and test.
Solution: Check that the unique values of the target variable are consistent. Use .unique() to check.

Error: Predictions with only one class
Cause: Highly imbalanced dataset or poorly calibrated threshold.
Solution: Adjust the scale_pos_weight parameter and review the cutoff threshold.

Error: ROC curve very close to reference line
Cause: Model unable to separate classes, likely due to lack of

signal in features.

Solution: Reevaluate feature engineering and explore transformed variables.

Error: AUC metric inconsistent with observed precision
Cause: AUC evaluates overall separation, while precision depends on the threshold.
Solution: Calibrate the cutoff point according to the problem's needs and observe the impact on metrics.

Error: ConfusionMatrix with very high FP or FN
Cause: Fixed threshold inadequate for the business cost.
Solution: Use predict_proba() and adjust the cutoff according to the business context.

Best Practices

- Use predict_proba() for more refined and calibrated decisions

- Calculate multiple metrics (Precision, Recall, F1, AUC) for holistic evaluation

- Adjust scale_pos_weight in imbalanced datasets to give weight to the minority class

- Visualize the ROC curve to understand the model's discriminatory capacity
- Use cross-validation with StratifiedKFold for greater reliability of results

Strategic Summary

Binary classification with XGBoost offers one of the best performances available in supervised model engineering. With flexibility to adjust thresholds, support for probabilistic metrics, and native features to handle imbalance, XGBClassifier is an essential tool in critical decision pipelines. Understanding how to adjust the model, calibrate probability, and interpret the output based on curves and metrics ensures not only technical performance but also operational reliability in production environments.

CHAPTER 7. FEATURE IMPORTANCE

XGBoost offers native mechanisms to calculate and visualize the importance of features in trained models, enabling informed decisions about feature engineering, variable selection, and model explainability. The analysis of feature importance is fundamental in applications that require transparency, such as credit, healthcare, and compliance. This chapter demonstrates how to extract, interpret, and visualize the three main importance criteria used by XGBoost — gain, cover, and frequency — as well as strategies to identify and remove redundant variables, strengthening model performance and interpretability.

After training the model with XGBClassifier or XGBRegressor, it is possible to directly access feature importance values:

python

```
model = XGBClassifier(use_label_encoder=False,
eval_metric='logloss')

model.fit(X_train, y_train)

importances =
model.get_booster().get_score(importance_type='gain')
```

The parameter importance_type defines the criterion used. There are three main options:

- Gain: average information gain obtained when the feature

is used for a split.

- Cover: average number of samples covered by splits using the feature.

- Frequency (or weight): number of times the feature was used in splits.

These measures offer different perspectives. Gain is more indicative of the actual contribution to improving the tree. Cover helps understand the reach of the feature. Frequency can be biased by features with many discrete values.

It is possible to list all importances directly:

python

```
gain = model.get_booster().get_score(importance_type='gain')

cover = model.get_booster().get_score(importance_type='cover')

freq = model.get_booster().get_score(importance_type='weight')
```

The visualization of importances is done with the plot_importance function from the library itself:

python

```
from xgboost import plot_importance

import matplotlib.pyplot as plt


plot_importance(model, importance_type='gain', title='Feature Importance - Gain')

plt.show()
```

This approach generates an ordered graph with the most relevant features at the top. The importance type can be alternated according to the analysis objective.

Another useful format is the manual bar chart for greater customization:

python

```python
import pandas as pd


importancia_df = pd.DataFrame(gain.items(),
columns=['Feature', 'Gain'])
importancia_df = importancia_df.sort_values(by='Gain',
ascending=False)


plt.barh(importancia_df['Feature'], importancia_df['Gain'])
plt.xlabel('Information Gain')
plt.title('Feature Importance - Gain')
plt.gca().invert_yaxis()
plt.show()
```

The analysis of importance may indicate features that are being underutilized or have no real impact on the model. In these cases, it is recommended to exclude them, provided the decision is validated by post-training metrics.

The elimination of variables should follow a careful approach. Simply excluding rarely used features may result in performance loss if there is interaction between variables. The ideal method is to test with different subsets and evaluate the impact on the metrics.

It is possible to manually exclude based on a minimum threshold:

python

```
limiar = 0.01

features_relevantes = [f for f, g in gain.items() if g > limiar]

X_train_filtrado = pd.DataFrame(X_train,
columns=feature_names)[features_relevantes]

X_test_filtrado = pd.DataFrame(X_test,
columns=feature_names)[features_relevantes]
```

This process can be iterated with GridSearchCV or cross-validation, maintaining stable performance and a leaner model.

Another advanced form of analysis is using interpretability libraries such as SHAP (SHapley Additive exPlanations), which offer local and global explanations of each feature's importance for individual predictions:

python

```
import shap


explainer = shap.Explainer(model)

shap_values = explainer(X_test)


shap.plots.beeswarm(shap_values)
```

The beeswarm plot shows the distribution of each feature's impact, including the sign (positive or negative) and magnitude. This approach is ideal when you want to justify the model's decision for a specific individual, such as in a credit score.

Additionally, the use of SHAP can reveal features with low global importance but high local impact — useful for segmentations or personalized recommendations.

For production projects, it is recommended to create automatic feature importance analysis pipelines, with logging of gain values across different training cycles, enabling auditability and traceability.

Common Error Resolution

Error: KeyError when accessing feature names
Cause: The model was trained with NumPy arrays without column names.
Solution: Use pandas.DataFrame with column names or manually map indices to names.

Error: All importance values returned are very low
Cause: Dataset with high noise level or non-informative features.
Solution: Perform correlation analysis, remove constant or irrelevant columns.

Error: Importance plot shows no features
Cause: Model not trained or importances not updated.
Solution: Check if model.fit() was executed correctly before extraction.

Error: Wrong interpretation of frequency importance
Cause: Use of the 'weight' metric without considering split quality.
Solution: Prioritize the 'gain' metric to assess the real impact of features.

Error: Performance drop after variable exclusion
Cause: Removal of variables with synergy among themselves.
Solution: Validate exclusion with multiple metrics and re-

evaluate feature engineering.

Best Practices

- Prioritize the 'gain' metric for decisions about feature removal

- Visualize different types of importance for a complete view

- Use plot_importance() and customized graphs for technical analysis

- Avoid manual exclusions without cross-validation and performance checking

- Integrate SHAP for explanatory interpretations in sensitive projects

Strategic Summary

Analyzing feature importance in XGBoost models is an essential step to ensure interpretability, efficiency, and robustness. Using metrics such as gain, cover, and frequency allows the developer to understand how the model is making decisions, identify irrelevant features, and refine the attribute set for new training cycles. Tools like SHAP extend the capacity for explanation, reinforcing business confidence in the predictions generated. A model that understands its own decisions is not only more efficient but also more defensible in regulatory and operational environments.

CHAPTER 8. OVERFITTING CONTROL

Although XGBoost is one of the most powerful machine learning libraries, it is also susceptible to overfitting — when the model learns too much from the training set patterns and loses its ability to generalize to new data. Controlling this phenomenon is essential to obtaining stable, efficient, and reliable models. This chapter presents the main overfitting mitigation strategies within the XGBoost ecosystem, focusing on early stopping, L1 and L2 regularization, and effective cross-validation techniques that ensure the robustness of the machine learning pipeline.

One of the most direct and effective ways to control overfitting in XGBoost is by using the early_stopping_rounds parameter, which stops training as soon as the model stops improving on a validation set. This prevents the algorithm from overfitting to the training data.

python

```
from sklearn.model_selection import train_test_split

from xgboost import XGBClassifier


X_train_full, X_valid, y_train_full, y_valid = train_test_split(X, y, test_size=0.3, random_state=42)


model = XGBClassifier(n_estimators=500, learning_rate=0.05, use_label_encoder=False, eval_metric='logloss')
```

```
model.fit(
    X_train_full, y_train_full,
    early_stopping_rounds=20,
    eval_set=[(X_valid, y_valid)],
    verbose=False
)
```

By using this parameter, the model stops training when the monitored metric on the validation set does not improve for 20 consecutive rounds. This reduces training time, saves computational resources, and improves the model's generalization ability.

Another efficient control mechanism is the use of L1 and L2 regularization. These techniques penalize model complexity, limiting its ability to overfit the data. In XGBoost, the parameters reg_alpha (L1) and reg_lambda (L2) allow direct control:

python

```
model = XGBClassifier(
    n_estimators=300,
    learning_rate=0.1,
    max_depth=5,
    reg_alpha=0.5,  # L1 Regularization
    reg_lambda=1.0, # L2 Regularization
    use_label_encoder=False,
    eval_metric='logloss'
)
```

```python
model.fit(X_train_full, y_train_full)
```

L1 regularization forces less relevant coefficients to become zero, promoting an implicit form of feature selection. L2 regularization smooths extreme coefficients, favoring simpler and more generalizable models.

These parameters must be adjusted based on experimentation, preferably combined with cross-validation to ensure result stability.

Cross-validation is another essential technique to combat overfitting. By splitting the data into multiple folds and testing the model on each, a reliable measure of predictive capacity is obtained. In XGBoost, cross-validation can be performed with cross_val_score or the native xgb.cv function:

python

```python
import xgboost as xgb

from sklearn.model_selection import StratifiedKFold


dtrain = xgb.DMatrix(X, label=y)
params = {
    'max_depth': 4,
    'eta': 0.1,
    'objective': 'binary:logistic',
    'eval_metric': 'auc',
    'reg_alpha': 0.5,
    'reg_lambda': 1.0
}
```

```
cv_result = xgb.cv(
    params=params,
    dtrain=dtrain,
    num_boost_round=200,
    nfold=5,
    early_stopping_rounds=15,
    seed=42,
    as_pandas=True
)
print(cv_result)
```

This approach returns metrics from each validation round, allowing the exact point where the model reaches its best performance before overfitting to be detected. Combining xgb.cv with early_stopping_rounds provides a powerful diagnostic mechanism.

Moreover, the choice of hyperparameters also directly impacts the risk of overfitting. Parameters that increase model complexity should be adjusted carefully:

- max_depth: the higher, the greater the chance of overfitting

- min_child_weight: higher values reduce splits on small regions

- subsample: controls the proportion of rows used per tree

- colsample_bytree: controls the proportion of columns

used per tree

- gamma: requires a minimum gain to allow a split

Adjusting these parameters in a balanced way is crucial to limiting complexity without compromising predictive capacity.

It is also possible to visualize the model's behavior over iterations with the evals_result log:

python

```python
model = XGBClassifier(n_estimators=200, eval_metric='logloss', use_label_encoder=False)

eval_set = [(X_train_full, y_train_full), (X_valid, y_valid)]


model.fit(
    X_train_full, y_train_full,
    eval_set=eval_set,
    early_stopping_rounds=20,
    verbose=False
)


results = model.evals_result()
import matplotlib.pyplot as plt


epochs = len(results['validation_0']['logloss'])
x_axis = range(0, epochs)
```

```
plt.plot(x_axis, results['validation_0']['logloss'], label='Training')
plt.plot(x_axis, results['validation_1']['logloss'],
label='Validation')
plt.xlabel('Iterations')
plt.ylabel('Log Loss')
plt.legend()
plt.title('Log Loss per Iteration')
plt.show()
```

This graph allows a visual assessment of when the model starts overfitting the training data, clearly showing the benefit of early stopping.

Another practical recommendation is to limit the number of estimators (n_estimators) when learning_rate is high. Conversely, when learning_rate is low, the number of trees can be increased without compromising generalization, provided early_stopping_rounds is active.

Finally, it is important to remember that overfitting can be related to dataset quality. Highly correlated features, very small datasets, or high noise levels can amplify the risk even when control techniques are applied.

Common Error Resolution

Error: Overfitting detected by validation metrics
Cause: Number of estimators too high or absence of regularization.
Solution: Activate early_stopping_rounds, adjust learning_rate, reg_alpha, and reg_lambda.

Error: Training logloss much lower than validation logloss
Cause: Model memorizing the training set.
Solution: Reduce max_depth, apply subsample, and validate with xgb.cv.

Error: High error when using the model on new data
Cause: Lack of cross-validation during tuning.
Solution: Use cross_val_score or xgb.cv with multiple folds.

Error: Early stopping not triggered despite no visible improvement
Cause: early_stopping_rounds configured, but eval_set not defined.
Solution: Explicitly define the validation set in the .fit() method.

Error: Performance drop after activating regularization
Cause: Excessive model penalization.
Solution: Adjust reg_alpha and reg_lambda progressively.

Best Practices

- Activate early_stopping_rounds whenever possible with eval_set

- Apply xgb.cv to validate model stability with multiple folds

- Control max_depth, min_child_weight, and gamma to limit complexity

- Adjust reg_alpha and reg_lambda to avoid overfitting without eliminating predictive capacity

- Visualize the logloss curve to identify the ideal stopping point

Strategic Summary

Controlling overfitting in XGBoost models is a decisive advantage for delivering stable and scalable solutions. Using early stopping, regularization, and cross-validation ensures that models maintain high performance without compromising generalization. More than avoiding errors, these techniques form the foundation of a professional and predictable modeling cycle, ready to be integrated into production systems, automated pipelines, and high-demand applications.

CHAPTER 9. ESSENTIAL HYPERPARAMETERS

The performance of any model based on XGBoost is strongly tied to the configuration of its hyperparameters. Correctly setting values for n_estimators, learning_rate, max_depth, and other critical parameters is decisive for achieving a balance between predictive performance, robustness, and computational cost. This chapter presents the most relevant hyperparameters of XGBoost, explaining their direct impacts on model behavior, the trade-offs involved, and how to perform manual and automatic tuning safely and efficiently.

The number of estimators (n_estimators) represents the total number of trees that will be trained sequentially. Each tree incrementally contributes to improving the model by correcting the errors of the previous tree. In general, higher values allow greater predictive capacity, provided they are combined with a proportionally lower learning_rate to avoid overfitting:

python

```
from xgboost import XGBClassifier


modelo = XGBClassifier(n_estimators=500, learning_rate=0.05, use_label_encoder=False, eval_metric='logloss')

modelo.fit(X_train, y_train)
```

A model with many estimators and a high learning_rate tends to quickly overfit the data. Therefore, n_estimators should always be calibrated together with learning_rate.

The learning_rate controls how strongly each new tree influences the final prediction. Lower values require more trees for convergence but offer greater stability and lower risk of overfitting. Higher values speed up learning but can result in unstable and overfitted models:

python

```
modelo = XGBClassifier(n_estimators=100, learning_rate=0.3,
use_label_encoder=False)

modelo.fit(X_train, y_train)
```

In real-world applications, values between 0.01 and 0.3 are most commonly used. When combined with early_stopping_rounds, it is possible to safely test lower learning_rates, allowing the model to stop automatically upon reaching the best performance.

The max_depth determines the maximum allowed depth for each tree. Deeper trees can capture complex patterns but also tend to memorize the data. Shallower trees are more generalist but less expressive. The ideal value depends on the dataset's complexity and the presence of non-linear interactions between variables:

python

```
modelo = XGBClassifier(max_depth=6, n_estimators=200,
learning_rate=0.1)

modelo.fit(X_train, y_train)
```

For common tabular data, values between 3 and 10 are considered stable. Beyond that, the chance of overfitting grows exponentially. Using min_child_weight and gamma also helps regularize very deep trees.

In addition to the three central parameters, XGBoost provides several other hyperparameters that directly affect model behavior:

- subsample: percentage of rows used per tree. Reduces overfitting.

- colsample_bytree: percentage of columns used per tree. Controls diversity.

- min_child_weight: minimum number of samples per leaf. Prevents splits on small regions.

- gamma: minimum gain required to allow a split. Penalizes irrelevant splits.

- reg_alpha and reg_lambda: L1 and L2 regularization weights.

These parameters act as model stabilizers, promoting simpler trees and predictions less prone to fluctuations.

Manual hyperparameter tuning can be performed iteratively, combining experimentation with problem knowledge. Below, a practical example of progressive tuning:

python

```python
# Step 1: reduce overfitting with regularization
modelo = XGBClassifier(
    max_depth=6,
    learning_rate=0.1,
    n_estimators=500,
    subsample=0.8,
```

```
    colsample_bytree=0.8,

    reg_alpha=0.5,

    reg_lambda=1.0

)

modelo.fit(X_train, y_train)
```

This configuration already establishes a more stable model. From this point, small adjustments can be made and impacts evaluated with cross-validation.

For more demanding projects, the use of automatic tuning is recommended. The two most common approaches are GridSearchCV and RandomizedSearchCV from scikit-learn. GridSearch tests all possible combinations, while RandomizedSearch selects random combinations within a defined space, being more efficient for large datasets:

python

```
from sklearn.model_selection import GridSearchCV


param_grid = {

    'max_depth': [3, 5, 7],

    'learning_rate': [0.01, 0.05, 0.1],

    'n_estimators': [100, 200, 500]

}


modelo_base = XGBClassifier(use_label_encoder=False,
eval_metric='logloss')

grid = GridSearchCV(modelo_base, param_grid,
```

```
scoring='roc_auc', cv=3, verbose=1)
grid.fit(X_train, y_train)
print("Best parameters:", grid.best_params_)
```

To save time and computation, RandomizedSearchCV can be used with n_iter=10 to test 10 random combinations:

python

```
from sklearn.model_selection import RandomizedSearchCV
from scipy.stats import randint, uniform


param_dist = {
    'max_depth': randint(3, 10),
    'learning_rate': uniform(0.01, 0.2),
    'n_estimators': randint(100, 500)
}


random_search    =    RandomizedSearchCV(modelo_base,
param_dist, n_iter=10, scoring='roc_auc', cv=3, verbose=1)
random_search.fit(X_train, y_train)
```

This automated process saves time and helps identify combinations that would not be manually tested.

The use of these tools should always be accompanied by cross-validation and metric verification with separate data to avoid overfitting during tuning.

After tuning, the model can be re-evaluated on the test set and integrated into the full pipeline, with clear performance metrics and reproducible settings.

Common Error Resolution

Error: Overfitting even with regularization activated
Cause: Poorly calibrated max_depth or learning_rate.
Solution: Reduce max_depth and test a lower learning_rate with higher n_estimators.

Error: Model very slow to train
Cause: High number of estimators without early stopping.
Solution: Activate early_stopping_rounds and monitor validation metrics.

Error: RandomizedSearchCV returning poor models
Cause: Poorly defined search space or too few iterations.
Solution: Increase n_iter and adjust parameter ranges based on preliminary tests.

Error: GridSearchCV taking hours to finish
Cause: Too many parameter combinations and high folds.
Solution: Reduce search space or use RandomizedSearchCV.

Error: Tuned parameters cause performance drop on test set
Cause: Overfitting to the training set during tuning.
Solution: Evaluate performance with cross_val_score and reserve an external validation set.

Best Practices

- Adjust learning_rate to low values and increase n_estimators proportionally
- Limit max_depth between 3 and 7 for common tabular data

- Use subsample and colsample_bytree to diversify trees

- Activate early_stopping_rounds whenever possible to

avoid unnecessary cycles

- Use automatic tuning with cross-validation for fine and efficient adjustments

Strategic Summary

XGBoost hyperparameters are the most powerful control point for transforming a basic model into a high-performance solution. Understanding the direct impact of each parameter, applying progressive adjustments, and combining cross-validation with automatic tuning ensures consistent and reliable results. The balance between expressiveness and generalization is what separates a stable model from a volatile solution. Mastering these configurations strengthens the technical foundation of any data scientist or machine learning engineer, enabling precise, efficient, and predictable deliveries.

CHAPTER 10. OPTIMIZATION WITH GRIDSEARCHCV

The search for the ideal hyperparameter configuration is a critical step in modeling with XGBoost. GridSearchCV, available in the scikit-learn library, allows automating this process systematically and reproducibly. It evaluates all possible combinations of a predefined set of parameters, using cross-validation to measure the performance of each configuration. This chapter presents the complete integration between XGBoost and GridSearchCV, including its use in pipelines with preprocessing and the definition of custom metrics to optimize the model according to the specific criteria of the problem.

The basis for using GridSearchCV is the compatibility between XGBClassifier or XGBRegressor and the scikit-learn API. This allows them to be integrated directly into automated searches:

python

```python
from xgboost import XGBClassifier

from sklearn.model_selection import GridSearchCV


model = XGBClassifier(use_label_encoder=False,
eval_metric='logloss')


param_grid = {
    'max_depth': [3, 5, 7],
```

```
    'learning_rate': [0.01, 0.05, 0.1],
    'n_estimators': [100, 200]
}


grid_search = GridSearchCV(model, param_grid,
scoring='roc_auc', cv=3, verbose=1)
grid_search.fit(X_train, y_train)
```

The param_grid defines the search space, while scoring determines the evaluation metric and cv the number of cross-validation folds. The verbose parameter controls the level of detail shown in the terminal during execution.

After tuning, it is possible to access the best parameters and the adjusted model directly:

python

```
print("Best parameters:", grid_search.best_params_)
melhor_modelo = grid_search.best_estimator_
```

In real projects, data rarely arrives ready for the model. It is common to need to apply transformations like encoding, normalization, and imputation of missing values. The scikit-learn Pipeline allows chaining these steps with the final model, facilitating both reproducibility and integration with GridSearchCV.

python

```
from sklearn.pipeline import Pipeline
from sklearn.preprocessing import StandardScaler
from sklearn.impute import SimpleImputer
```

```
pipeline = Pipeline([
    ('imputer', SimpleImputer(strategy='mean')),
    ('scaler', StandardScaler()),
    ('xgb', XGBClassifier(use_label_encoder=False,
eval_metric='logloss'))
])

param_grid = {
    'xgb__max_depth': [3, 5],
    'xgb__learning_rate': [0.1, 0.05],
    'xgb__n_estimators': [100, 200]
}

grid = GridSearchCV(pipeline, param_grid, scoring='roc_auc',
cv=3)
grid.fit(X_train, y_train)
```

When using a Pipeline, the parameter names must be prefixed with the step name (xgb__, scaler__, imputer__, etc.). This ensures that GridSearchCV can correctly manipulate the internal components of the pipeline.

In many scenarios, it is necessary to use specific metrics to capture business nuances. For example, when the priority is to minimize false negatives, a metric based on recall may be more appropriate than accuracy or AUC. GridSearchCV allows the use of custom evaluation functions via make_scorer:

python

```
from sklearn.metrics import make_scorer, f1_score


f1 = make_scorer(f1_score)


grid = GridSearchCV(model, param_grid, scoring=f1, cv=3)
grid.fit(X_train, y_train)
```

It is also possible to define a custom scoring function that considers multiple metrics or specific penalties. The function must receive y_true and y_pred as arguments and return a numeric value:

python

```
from sklearn.metrics import precision_score


def custom_metric(y_true, y_pred):
    return 0.7 * precision_score(y_true, y_pred) + 0.3 *
f1_score(y_true, y_pred)


custom_scorer = make_scorer(custom_metric)


grid = GridSearchCV(model, param_grid,
scoring=custom_scorer, cv=3)
grid.fit(X_train, y_train)
```

This type of control is fundamental when standard metrics do not reflect the real priorities of the project.

During GridSearchCV execution, each parameter combination is tested on multiple data splits. This can generate hundreds or thousands of executions, depending on the size of the search space. Therefore, it is essential to define the parameter space intelligently, avoiding redundant tests or unviable combinations.

Another important point is the external validation of the final model. Even after identifying the best combination of parameters, it is recommended to test the adjusted model on a separate dataset to verify its generalization:

python

```
from sklearn.metrics import classification_report


y_pred_final = grid.best_estimator_.predict(X_test)
print(classification_report(y_test, y_pred_final))
```

This step ensures that the model did not benefit only from cross-validation but maintains performance on completely new data.

For in-depth analysis, cv_results_ provides access to all metrics obtained during the search:

python

```
import pandas as pd


resultados = pd.DataFrame(grid.cv_results_)
print(resultados[['params', 'mean_test_score',
'rank_test_score']])
```

This data can be exported and analyzed to understand the model's behavior throughout the search space, identifying patterns, bottlenecks, and more promising hyperparameter ranges for future testing.

When well used, GridSearchCV elevates the maturity level of any machine learning project, offering a systematic and reliable method for tuning, evaluation, and model selection. Its use with pipelines and custom metrics further strengthens the ability to adapt to project needs.

Common Error Resolution

Error: ValueError when using Pipeline with GridSearchCV
Cause: Misdefined parameters without step prefix.
Solution: Prefix with xgb__, scaler__, etc., according to the step name in the pipeline.

Error: Extremely slow GridSearch execution
Cause: Very large search space with a high number of folds.
Solution: Reduce the parameter grid or use RandomizedSearchCV with n_iter.

Error: Optimal result with poor performance on test set
Cause: Overfitting during the tuning process.
Solution: Validate the final model on an external set and review the metrics used.

Error: TypeError when passing custom function
Cause: Metric function with wrong signature.
Solution: Ensure the function receives y_true and y_pred and returns a float.

Error: GridSearchCV does not improve performance
Cause: Poorly chosen search space or already saturated model.
Solution: Redefine the search ranges based on previous analyses

or add new features.

Best Practices

- Chain preprocessing steps with Pipeline to maintain reproducibility

- Correctly prefix parameters when using GridSearchCV with pipeline

- First test with small grids before scaling the search space

- Validate the adjusted model with an external set to measure generalization

- Use custom metrics with make_scorer to tailor the model to the real problem

Strategic Summary

Optimization with GridSearchCV transforms hyperparameter tuning into a systematic, results-oriented process. By integrating it with pipelines and custom metrics, it is possible to align the model with the specific objectives of the project with maximum precision and control. This approach not only improves model performance but also professionalizes technical delivery, making it more predictable, auditable, and replicable across different development cycles. Mastery of this resource is essential for any professional who aims to operate with excellence in machine learning projects with XGBoost.

CHAPTER 11. USING RANDOMIZEDSEARCHCV

Hyperparameter optimization is one of the most critical steps for the final performance of XGBoost-based models. Finding effective combinations of parameters such as max_depth, learning_rate, n_estimators, subsample, and colsample_bytree can substantially improve the predictive capacity, generalization, and computational efficiency of the model. While GridSearchCV performs an exhaustive search over a grid of predefined values, RandomizedSearchCV explores random combinations within specific distributions, reducing computational cost and accelerating the tuning process without losing optimization effectiveness.

RandomizedSearchCV is especially recommended in situations where the search space is large, execution time is restricted, or there is no clear understanding of the best ranges for each hyperparameter. Instead of testing all possibilities like in GridSearchCV, it selects random combinations based on the provided distributions, respecting a maximum number of iterations defined by the user.

python

```
from xgboost import XGBClassifier
from sklearn.model_selection import RandomizedSearchCV
from scipy.stats import uniform, randint

modelo = XGBClassifier(use_label_encoder=False,
```

```
eval_metric='logloss')

parametros = {
    'max_depth': randint(3, 10),
    'learning_rate': uniform(0.01, 0.3),
    'n_estimators': randint(100, 500),
    'subsample': uniform(0.6, 0.4),
    'colsample_bytree': uniform(0.6, 0.4),
    'gamma': uniform(0, 1),
    'reg_alpha': uniform(0, 1),
    'reg_lambda': uniform(0, 1)
}

busca = RandomizedSearchCV(
    modelo,
    param_distributions=parametros,
    n_iter=50,
    scoring='roc_auc',
    cv=3,
    verbose=1,
    random_state=42,
    n_jobs=-1
)

busca.fit(X_train, y_train)
```

```
melhor_modelo = busca.best_estimator_
```

The main advantage is the reduced execution time. With n_iter=50, the algorithm tests only 50 combinations among thousands of possibilities, offering competitive results at a much lower computational cost than an exhaustive search.

The choice of distributions for each hyperparameter is strategic. Randint distributions are appropriate for discrete parameters like max_depth and n_estimators. Uniform is ideal for continuous parameters like learning_rate, gamma, reg_alpha, and reg_lambda. The choice of limits should consider reasonable values based on practical experience, dataset size, and model behavior.

In addition to the performance gain in time, RandomizedSearchCV allows exploring parts of the search space that GridSearchCV would ignore by being restricted to fixed points. This can reveal unexpectedly effective combinations, especially in models with many interdependent hyperparameters.

Another important use is as a preliminary step for a second, more refined tuning phase. RandomizedSearchCV can be used to delimit a promising region of the parameter space and then apply GridSearchCV in that narrower region, with fewer combinations and greater precision.

RandomizedSearchCV accepts cross-validation via cv, multiple metrics by scoring, and can operate in parallel with n_jobs=-1, leveraging all available cores of the machine. This makes it applicable in notebooks, servers, or automated pipelines with CI/CD.

To visualize the results of all tested combinations, you can extract cv_results_ as a DataFrame and sort by the metrics:

python

```
import pandas as pd

resultados = pd.DataFrame(busca.cv_results_)
resultados_ordenados =
resultados.sort_values(by='mean_test_score', ascending=False)
print(resultados_ordenados[['params',
'mean_test_score']].head())
```

This allows inspecting trends, such as model sensitivity to certain parameters, overfitting behavior, and the influence of regularization.

Even with its effectiveness, the use of RandomizedSearchCV requires caution. Poorly calibrated distributions or irrelevant ranges can lead to unviable or unhelpful parameter combinations. It is important to understand the effects of each hyperparameter in XGBoost and adjust limits based on technical analysis, not blind trial and error.

Another essential point is to fix the random seed (random_state) to ensure reproducibility, especially in projects that require documentation or validation by technical audit.

Common Error Resolution

Error: ValueError: Continuous is not supported for max_depth
Cause: Use of uniform distribution for an integer parameter.
Solution: Replace with randint for parameters like max_depth and n_estimators.

Error: long execution time or freezing
Cause: High number of combinations or n_iter too high.
Solution: Reduce n_iter or optimize distributions for more relevant regions.

Error: best_score_ much lower than expected
Cause: Poorly defined search space covering weak parameters.
Solution: Adjust limits and test distribution focused on more productive intervals.

Error: Type incompatibility using uniform with boolean parameters
Cause: Inadequate distribution definition for a binary parameter.
Solution: Define fixed values or explicit list with choices and np.random.choice().

Error: inconsistency in results between runs
Cause: Lack of random_state or uncontrolled multithread environment.
Solution: Set random seed and ensure isolation of experiments.

Best Practices

- Use RandomizedSearchCV in projects with time constraints and extensive search spaces

- Define distributions consistent with the type and effect of each hyperparameter

- Fix random_state to ensure technical reproducibility

- Evaluate results with cv_results_ to adjust future strategies

- Integrate RandomizedSearchCV into automated pipelines and performance tests

Strategic Summary

RandomizedSearchCV is a valuable tool for efficient

hyperparameter tuning in XGBoost projects. With its non-exhaustive approach and flexibility in search distributions, it allows exploring the parameter space at a lower computational cost with great potential for discovering good configurations. When used with technical criteria and aligned with the model's objective, it represents a practical advancement in the operational maturity of modeling, reducing time, expanding scope, and delivering optimized solutions more quickly.

CHAPTER 12. ADVANCED MODEL EVALUATION

Correctly evaluating a machine learning model is as important as training it. In XGBoost-based classifiers, evaluation goes beyond accuracy: it involves analyzing the balance between errors, understanding how the model behaves at different thresholds, and visualizing its learning capacity throughout iterations. This chapter presents the most robust techniques for advanced model evaluation, including confusion matrix, metrics such as precision, recall, and F1 score, as well as learning curves, which are fundamental for tuning, comparing, and justifying models in technical and production environments.

The confusion matrix is the basic tool to interpret model behavior in binary classifications. It presents, in a cross table, the true positives, true negatives, false positives, and false negatives, allowing a detailed analysis of the errors committed.

python

```
from sklearn.metrics import confusion_matrix,
ConfusionMatrixDisplay


y_pred = model.predict(X_test)

cm = confusion_matrix(y_test, y_pred)


disp = ConfusionMatrixDisplay(confusion_matrix=cm)

disp.plot()
```

This graph reveals how the model is hitting or missing its predictions, separating errors by type. A balanced matrix with a high number of true positives and true negatives indicates a reliable classifier. A biased matrix may indicate problems such as poorly calibrated threshold, class imbalance, or overfitting.

To evaluate classification models, metrics derived from the confusion matrix are indispensable. The three main ones are:

- Precision: how many of the predicted positives are actually positives

- Recall: how many of the actual positives were correctly identified

- F1 Score: harmonic mean between precision and recall, balancing the two

These metrics are especially useful when the costs of errors are not symmetrical. In medical or fraud problems, underestimating is much more critical than overestimating.

python

```
from sklearn.metrics import classification_report,
precision_score, recall_score, f1_score


print(classification_report(y_test, y_pred))
```

To calculate manually and use in customized analyses:

python

```
precision = precision_score(y_test, y_pred)
```

```
recall = recall_score(y_test, y_pred)
f1 = f1_score(y_test, y_pred)


print("Precision:", precision)
print("Recall:", recall)
print("F1 Score:", f1)
```

These metrics must be interpreted together. A model with high precision but low recall is correct when it predicts positive, but leaves many real positives out. A model with high recall and low precision predicts many false positives. The ideal balance depends on the business context.

Another fundamental component of advanced evaluation is the analysis of the learning curve. It shows how the model evolves with more data or more iterations, allowing the detection of overfitting, underfitting, and identifying if the model has already reached its learning limit.

python

```
import matplotlib.pyplot as plt
from sklearn.model_selection import learning_curve
from sklearn.model_selection import StratifiedKFold


cv = StratifiedKFold(n_splits=5, shuffle=True,
random_state=42)


train_sizes, train_scores, test_scores = learning_curve(
    model, X, y, cv=cv, scoring='f1', n_jobs=-1,
```

```
    train_sizes=[0.1, 0.3, 0.5, 0.7, 1.0]
)


train_scores_mean = train_scores.mean(axis=1)
test_scores_mean = test_scores.mean(axis=1)


plt.plot(train_sizes, train_scores_mean, label="Training")
plt.plot(train_sizes, test_scores_mean, label="Validation")
plt.xlabel("Training set size")
plt.ylabel("F1 Score")
plt.title("Learning Curve")
plt.legend()
plt.show()
```

If the training curve is much higher than the validation curve with a stable gap, the model is suffering from overfitting. If both are low, there is underfitting. Ideally, the curves should converge or maintain a short distance, indicating stable learning.

Another important use of the learning curve is to decide whether it is worth collecting more data. If performance continues to rise with more samples, the effort may be worthwhile. If the curve stabilizes, the problem may be in the hyperparameters or feature engineering.

In addition, XGBoost allows direct monitoring of metric evolution throughout iterations with evals_result, generating convergence graphs by metric:

python

```
results = model.evals_result()

epochs = len(results['validation_0']['logloss'])
x_axis = range(0, epochs)


plt.plot(x_axis, results['validation_0']['logloss'], label='Training')
plt.plot(x_axis, results['validation_1']['logloss'],
label='Validation')
plt.xlabel('Iterations')
plt.ylabel('Log Loss')
plt.title('Log Loss Convergence')
plt.legend()
plt.show()
```

This type of graph is essential for tuning and hyperparameter adjustment, helping to visualize the real impact of each configuration on model behavior over time.

Performance analysis should not stop at the numbers. It is fundamental to segment results by interest groups, probability ranges, or specific categories. This can reveal unwanted behaviors, such as bias against certain groups or inconsistency in minority classes.

Below, an example of segmentation by predicted probability range:

python

```
import pandas as pd
```

```
df_resultados = pd.DataFrame({'real': y_test, 'proba':
model.predict_proba(X_test)[:, 1]})

df_resultados['range'] = pd.cut(df_resultados['proba'], bins=[0,
0.3, 0.7, 1], labels=['low', 'medium', 'high'])


print(df_resultados.groupby('range')['real'].mean())
```

This analysis allows calibrating the model's confidence in different scenarios, adjusting the decision threshold or applying specific strategies by probability range.

Common Error Resolution

Error: F1 score very low despite good accuracy
Cause: Imbalanced classes or inadequate threshold.
Solution: Use recall- and precision-based metrics. Adjust decision threshold with predict_proba().

Error: Confusion matrix with excessive false negatives
Cause: Model with low recall or very conservative threshold.
Solution: Lower threshold, use recall_score as main metric.

Error: Learning curve with fixed gap between training and validation
Cause: Persistent overfitting.
Solution: Apply regularization, reduce max_depth, use early_stopping_rounds.

Error: Inconsistent metrics between validation and test
Cause: Poorly applied cross-validation or non-stratified data.
Solution: Use StratifiedKFold and ensure controlled randomness in splits.

Error: Flat learning curve with low performance
Cause: Model unable to learn relevant patterns.
Solution: Reevaluate feature engineering, test other algorithms, or increase data volume.

Best Practices

- Calculate precision, recall, and f1_score whenever there are imbalanced classes

- Use confusion matrix as a visual tool for error interpretation

- Plot learning curves to understand model behavior with more data

- Validate models with StratifiedKFold to maintain class proportions

- Segment predictions by probability ranges for calibration analyses

Strategic Summary

Advanced evaluation of models with XGBoost requires more than just looking at accuracy. Metrics like precision, recall, and F1 provide deep insights into the model's errors and successes. The confusion matrix allows interpreting these errors in detail, while learning curves show the model's evolution path and reveal when it has learned all it could. By combining these tools with probability segmentations and rigorous validations, it is possible to elevate the analysis to a professional level, ensuring not only technical performance but also security and confidence in the automated decisions generated by the model.

CHAPTER 13. MULTICLASS MODELS WITH XGBOOST

Building multiclass classification models is a recurring need in real-world applications, such as product classification, transaction types, customer profiles, or multiple diagnoses. XGBoost offers full support for multiclass tasks, with optimized strategies, specific parameter adjustments, and metrics adapted for multiple categories. This chapter presents the practical use of XGBoost in classifications with more than two classes, addressing the one-vs-rest and softmax strategies, precise hyperparameter tuning, and evaluation with metrics dedicated to multiclass scenarios.

To perform multiclass classification with XGBoost, it is necessary to configure the parameter objective='multi:softprob' or objective='multi:softmax', and indicate the total number of classes with num_class.

- multi:softprob: returns probabilities for each class.

- multi:softmax: directly returns the class with the highest probability.

Below, an example using the digits dataset from the sklearn library, which contains images of digits from 0 to 9, totaling 10 classes:

python

```
from sklearn.datasets import load_digits
from sklearn.model_selection import train_test_split
```

```python
from xgboost import XGBClassifier

X, y = load_digits(return_X_y=True)
X_train, X_test, y_train, y_test = train_test_split(X, y,
test_size=0.2, random_state=42)

model = XGBClassifier(
    objective='multi:softprob',
    num_class=10,
    eval_metric='mlogloss',
    use_label_encoder=False
)
model.fit(X_train, y_train)
```

In this mode, the output of predict_proba will be a matrix with 10 columns, one for each class. The class with the highest value per row represents the final prediction.

To convert these probabilities into final labels:

python

```python
import numpy as np

y_pred_proba = model.predict_proba(X_test)
y_pred = np.argmax(y_pred_proba, axis=1)
```

The one-vs-rest strategy can also be applied using multiple instances of XGBClassifier via OneVsRestClassifier, allowing greater control over the individual behavior per class:

python

```
from sklearn.multiclass import OneVsRestClassifier


ovr_model =
OneVsRestClassifier(XGBClassifier(use_label_encoder=False,
eval_metric='logloss'))

ovr_model.fit(X_train, y_train)

y_pred = ovr_model.predict(X_test)
```

This approach is useful when differentiated strategies are desired per class, such as specific weights, thresholds, or independent regularizations.

In addition to defining objective and num_class, some hyperparameters require special attention in the multiclass context:

- eval_metric: mlogloss and merror are recommended for multiclass.

- scale_pos_weight: does not apply directly; specific weights must be made via sample_weight.

- use_label_encoder: always disabled to avoid warnings and unexpected behaviors.

In the multiclass context, the most useful metrics are:

- Accuracy: proportion of total hits over the dataset.

- Multiclass confusion matrix: shows errors among all possible class combinations.

- Macro F1 score: calculates the F1 score for each class and averages without weighting by frequency.

Weighted F1 score: calculates F1 for each class and averages weighted by the number of samples.

Multiclass Log Loss: heavily penalizes predictions with high confidence and error.

Below, practical application of these metrics:

python

```
from sklearn.metrics import accuracy_score,
classification_report, confusion_matrix


print("Accuracy:", accuracy_score(y_test, y_pred))

print(confusion_matrix(y_test, y_pred))

print(classification_report(y_test, y_pred))
```

The classification_report provides precision, recall, and F1 per class, in addition to macro and weighted values. This allows evaluating whether the model is performing well overall or only on more frequent classes.

The visualization of the confusion matrix is also possible in multiclass contexts:

python

```
from sklearn.metrics import ConfusionMatrixDisplay


disp = ConfusionMatrixDisplay.from_predictions(y_test,
y_pred)

disp.plot()
```

This graph is fundamental to detecting specific confusions, such as classes frequently confused with each other, and guiding preprocessing strategies, feature adjustments, or separation of close classes.

In multiclass tasks, probability analysis is also valid. The probabilities generated by predict_proba help to understand the model's confidence level for each class, which can be used to create decision rules or interfaces with more reliable feedback.

python

```
for i in range(5):
    print(f"Input {i}: Predicted class = {y_pred[i]}, Confidence =
{np.max(y_pred_proba[i]):.2f}")
```

The ROC curve and AUC are not directly applicable in multiclass tasks with more than two classes. For this, macro and micro-averaged versions of AUC are used with OneVsRestClassifier when necessary.

In computational terms, multiclass models tend to be more costly, both in training time and memory. The use of early_stopping_rounds and refined parameter tuning becomes even more essential to avoid overfitting and performance loss.

Common Error Resolution

Error: ValueError: num_class must be set for multi:softprob
Cause: Multiclass objective defined without indicating the number of classes.
Solution: Add num_class=value when instantiating the model.

Error: Output shape mismatch when using predict_proba
Cause: Attempt to use predict_proba with multi:softmax.

Solution: Switch to multi:softprob to obtain probabilities per class.

Error: Result with many confusions between close classes
Cause: Features with little discrimination between classes.
Solution: Reinforce feature engineering and apply importance analysis.

Error: Minority class with poor performance
Cause: Imbalance between classes in a multiclass task.
Solution: Apply class_weight in the pipeline, sample balancing, or OneVsRestClassifier.

Error: Good global performance but specific classes with very low F1
Cause: Evaluation only by accuracy without considering per-class metrics.
Solution: Use classification_report and macro and weighted F1 scores.

Best Practices

- Explicitly define objective='multi:softprob' and num_class in the model

- Use predict_proba for more reliable decisions and confidence analysis

- Evaluate with macro and weighted metrics to capture balanced performance among classes

- Visualize confusion matrix to detect class-specific error patterns

- Consider OneVsRestClassifier when each class requires individual treatment

Strategic Summary

XGBoost offers full support for multiclass tasks, enabling highly scalable and interpretable models even in scenarios with dozens of categories. With proper parameter tuning, strategic choice of objective, and use of dedicated metrics, it is possible to achieve precise and robust classifications. Understanding the impacts of multiclass modeling decisions — from encoding to evaluation — is what transforms a generic classifier into an applied, validated, and reliable solution for real-world production contexts.

CHAPTER 14. INTEGRATION WITH PANDAS AND NUMPY

XGBoost is highly compatible with widely used data structures in data science, such as NumPy arrays and Pandas DataFrames. This integration allows preparing, manipulating, transforming, and feeding models with great flexibility and control. This chapter presents the best practices for dataset handling using Pandas and NumPy, techniques for conversion between formats compatible with XGBoost, and fine adjustments to ensure optimal performance in reading, writing, and in-memory processing.

Most structured datasets used with XGBoost are in .csv, .xlsx, .parquet, or other tabular formats. Pandas is the most direct tool for initial reading and manipulation of these files:

python

```python
import pandas as pd


df = pd.read_csv('dados.csv')
print(df.head())
```

After reading, it is common to need to adjust columns, convert types, and handle missing data. These transformations should be done before feeding the model:

python

```python
df.drop(columns=['id', 'data_registro'], inplace=True)
df['categoria'] = df['categoria'].astype('category').cat.codes
df.fillna(df.median(), inplace=True)
```

When feeding the XGBoost model, it can accept both DataFrames and NumPy arrays. In both cases, the model internally converts them to DMatrix format, optimized for performance. Nevertheless, in applications more sensitive to time or memory, manual conversion to DMatrix can bring significant gains:

python

```python
import xgboost as xgb
import numpy as np


X = df.drop('target', axis=1).values
y = df['target'].values


dtrain = xgb.DMatrix(data=X, label=y)
```

When working directly with DMatrix, it is possible to pass additional metadata such as weights, labels, and missing value indicators:

python

```python
dtrain = xgb.DMatrix(data=X, label=y, weight=np.ones(len(y)),
missing=np.nan)
```

Despite supporting different structures, there are differences in

XGBoost behavior depending on the input data type. When the model receives a DataFrame, it preserves column names and uses them in feature importance reports. When it receives a NumPy array, identifiers are converted to f0, f1, f2, etc.:

python

```
from xgboost import XGBClassifier


model = XGBClassifier()
model.fit(X, y)


importances = model.feature_importances_
print(importances)
```

To maintain traceability between the original columns and numeric indices, it is recommended to always work with DataFrames or keep a mapping dictionary:

python

```
feature_names = df.drop(columns='target').columns
```

Conversion between Pandas and NumPy is straightforward. To convert a DataFrame into an array:

python

```
X_array = df.drop(columns='target').to_numpy()
```

To convert back:

python

```
df_novo = pd.DataFrame(X_array, columns=feature_names)
```

This cycle is useful when intermediate steps require faster mathematical operations with NumPy, such as normalizations, linear transformations, or vector manipulations:

python

```
X_normalizado = (X_array - X_array.mean(axis=0)) /
X_array.std(axis=0)
```

Reading and writing performance also impacts the development cycle with XGBoost. CSV files are easy to use but slow for reading at scale. Alternatives like .parquet or .feather are more recommended for large volumes:

python

```
df.to_parquet('dados.parquet')

df_rapido = pd.read_parquet('dados.parquet')
```

When working with large datasets, it is possible to load only parts into memory with chunksize:

python

```
for chunk in pd.read_csv('dados.csv', chunksize=10000):

    processar(chunk)
```

This approach prevents memory overflows in resource-limited environments, allowing scalable pipelines with XGBoost.

Another relevant point is type compatibility. Categorical columns need to be converted to numeric before training:

python

```python
df['tipo'] = df['tipo'].astype('category').cat.codes
```

For datasets with many null values, the replacement or removal strategy must be applied carefully. DMatrix handles missing values well, but Pandas and NumPy require filling for calculations and statistical operations:

python

```python
df.fillna(-999, inplace=True)
```

This practice should only be adopted cautiously and with impact tests, as it may induce the model to learn artificial patterns based on the imputation value.

In the validation and training process, the train-test split can be performed directly on DataFrames:

python

```python
from sklearn.model_selection import train_test_split

X = df.drop(columns='target')
y = df['target']
X_train, X_test, y_train, y_test = train_test_split(X, y, test_size=0.3, random_state=42)
```

After that, both arrays and DataFrames can be used to feed XGBClassifier, depending on the preprocessing pipeline adopted.

Common Error Resolution

Error: ValueError: could not convert string to float
Cause: Categorical or textual column not converted before training.
Solution: Apply numeric encoding before training with .astype('category').cat.codes.

Error: KeyError when accessing columns after conversion
Cause: Loss of column names when converting DataFrame to NumPy.
Solution: Keep a feature_names list separately to reverse conversions.

Error: CSV file too large causing memory crash
Cause: Full reading of the file without memory usage control.
Solution: Use chunksize in read_csv() to process in parts.

Error: Model with features named f0, f1, f2
Cause: Input in NumPy format without column names.
Solution: Use DataFrame to preserve metadata during training.

Error: TypeError when trying to save DMatrix with Pandas
Cause: Attempt to pass DataFrame directly to save_binary().
Solution: Convert to NumPy or DMatrix before export.

Best Practices

- Work with DataFrames whenever possible to maintain metadata

- Convert categorical columns to integers with .astype('category').cat.codes

- Use .parquet or .feather instead of .csv for fast large-scale reading

- Manually use DMatrix in projects focused on performance

- Control memory usage on large files with chunksize in read_csv()

Strategic Summary

The integration between XGBoost, Pandas, and NumPy forms the operational basis of any technical pipeline focused on performance and flexibility. Knowing when and how to convert between structures, preserve column names, and adjust formats allows building reliable, interpretable, and scalable workflows. Mastering these interactions reduces debugging time, improves model traceability, and accelerates the complete development cycle with machine learning.

CHAPTER 15. APPLICATIONS IN TIME SERIES

Although XGBoost is not a native library for time series, it can be highly effectively adapted for this type of problem through feature engineering techniques and strict control over the temporal split of the data. Time series are present in many real-world applications such as demand forecasting, pricing, energy consumption, operational metrics, and user behavior. For XGBoost to be used correctly in these contexts, it is essential to structure the dataset with time-based features, apply splits respecting temporal order, and interpret results with a focus on trend and seasonality. This chapter presents a practical, robust, and validated approach to working with time series using XGBoost.

The first step to applying XGBoost in time series is to transform the sequence into a tabular dataset by introducing lag features, which represent previous values of the series as inputs to the model. This allows the algorithm to learn historical patterns and make predictions based on the recent past.

Suppose a dataset of daily energy consumption:

python

```
import pandas as pd


df = pd.read_csv('energia.csv', parse_dates=['data'],
index_col='data')

df['consumo'] = df['consumo'].astype(float)
```

To transform the series into a supervised format, a sliding window with lags is created:

python

```
for lag in range(1, 8):
    df[f'lag_{lag}'] = df['consumo'].shift(lag)
```

In this example, the values lag_1 to lag_7 represent consumption over the previous 7 days. It is also possible to include moving averages, trend indicators, and seasonal features:

python

```
df['media_3'] = df['consumo'].rolling(3).mean()
df['dia_da_semana'] = df.index.dayofweek
```

After creating the features, it is necessary to remove the rows with null values resulting from shift and rolling operations:

python

```
df.dropna(inplace=True)
```

The split between training and testing in time series must not be random. The model must learn from past data and be tested on future data, respecting the sequential structure of time. This avoids data leakage and more faithfully simulates the real forecasting scenario.

python

```
limite = int(len(df) * 0.8)
```

```
X = df.drop(columns='consumo')
y = df['consumo']
```

```
X_train, X_test = X.iloc[:limite], X.iloc[limite:]
y_train, y_test = y.iloc[:limite], y.iloc[limite:]
```

Prediction with XGBoost follows the same structure as other models:

python

```
from xgboost import XGBRegressor
```

```
modelo = XGBRegressor(n_estimators=100, learning_rate=0.1)
modelo.fit(X_train, y_train)
y_pred = modelo.predict(X_test)
```

For evaluation, RMSE and MAE are used, metrics appropriate for forecasting continuous sequential values:

python

```
from sklearn.metrics import mean_absolute_error,
mean_squared_error
import numpy as np
```

```
rmse = np.sqrt(mean_squared_error(y_test, y_pred))
mae = mean_absolute_error(y_test, y_pred)
```

```
print("RMSE:", rmse)
print("MAE:", mae)
```

It is also useful to visualize the real versus predicted curve, aligning dates correctly:

python

```
import matplotlib.pyplot as plt


y_test_plot = y_test.copy()
y_test_plot[:] = y_pred


plt.figure(figsize=(15, 5))
plt.plot(y_test.index, y_test, label='Real')
plt.plot(y_test_plot.index, y_test_plot, label='Predicted')
plt.legend()
plt.title('Comparison Between Real and Predicted
Consumption')
plt.xlabel('Date')
plt.ylabel('Consumption')
plt.show()
```

This type of graph is essential to understand whether the model is correctly capturing trend, cycles, and peaks. In many cases, performance can be improved by combining short- and medium-term forecasts with techniques like stacking or ensemble with other models.

An advanced practice is recursive forecasting: using the model to predict one step ahead, then using that prediction as input to forecast the next point. This process requires strict control over real-time generated temporal attributes.

python

```
# Recursive forecast for the next 7 days
ultimo = X_test.iloc[-1:].copy()


for i in range(7):
    pred = modelo.predict(ultimo)[0]
    novo = ultimo.shift(-1, axis=1)
    novo.iloc[0, -1] = pred
    y_test_plot = pd.concat([y_test_plot, pd.Series([pred],
index=[y_test_plot.index[-1] + pd.Timedelta(days=1)])])
    ultimo = novo
```

This type of approach is useful in production systems that need to generate continuous sliding window forecasts in real time.

XGBoost can also incorporate exogenous variables into time series forecasting, such as economic indicators, weather variables, or external data that impact the target value. These should be included as additional columns in the original DataFrame.

In each new forecasting cycle, it is recommended to update the model with the most recent data and reevaluate performance to maintain accuracy over time.

Common Error Resolution

Error: ValueError when training with sequential data
Cause: Presence of NaNs after creating lags or rolling.
Solution: Apply dropna() after creating temporal features.

Error: Model performs well in training but fails in testing
Cause: Random split causing temporal data leakage.
Solution: Perform split based on increasing dates using iloc.

Error: Predictions with linear and unresponsive behavior
Cause: Insufficient lags or lack of seasonal features.
Solution: Include more lags, moving averages, and seasonal columns such as dayofweek.

Error: Sharp drop in accuracy in recursive forecasting
Cause: Error accumulation when using predictions as future inputs.
Solution: Reduce forecasting horizon or reevaluate feature engineering to stabilize the cycle.

Error: Incorrect alignment of forecast dates
Cause: Failure to associate Pandas indices with forecasts.
Solution: Maintain consistency between series indices and predictions.

Best Practices

- Create multiple lag features and moving averages to capture historical patterns

- Use dayofweek, month, is_weekend as seasonal attributes

- Make temporal splits with iloc or ordered date filters

- Visualize real vs. predicted graphs sequentially with dates on the axis

- Periodically update the model with the most recent data to maintain performance

Strategic Summary

XGBoost can be highly effectively applied to time series problems when supported by an appropriate structure of feature engineering and sequential control. The creation of sliding windows, the temporal segmentation of the data, and the use of seasonal variables elevate the model to a new level of predictive performance. By adapting your pipeline for this type of task, it is possible to extract reliable forecasts aligned with the operational demands of time-based businesses, maintaining full control over the data and model logic.

CHAPTER 16. INTERPRETATION WITH SHAP VALUES

The explainability of machine learning models has gained technical and institutional prominence, especially in applications where automated decisions affect people or critical processes. Although XGBoost is known for its performance, its internal behavior can be difficult to interpret without specific tools. SHAP (SHapley Additive exPlanations) offers a mathematically consistent and computationally viable way to interpret predictions of tree-based models like XGBoost. This chapter covers strategies to visualize feature impact, distinguish local and global explanations, and integrate these interpretations into operational dashboards.

SHAP assigns each feature an individual contribution to the prediction made by the model, based on an adaptation of Shapley values from game theory. This allows a prediction to be decomposed into a sum of positive and negative impacts, highlighting how each variable pushes the output up or down.

The shap library offers direct integration with XGBoost and can be installed via:

bash

```
pip install shap
```

After training an XGBoost model, the first step is to generate the explainer object compatible with the model:

python

```
import shap

explainer = shap.Explainer(model, X_train)
shap_values = explainer(X_test)
```

The shap_values object contains the individual contributions of each feature for each sample in the test set. The sum of the contributions plus the model's base value (average of predictions on the training set) results in the predicted value for each sample.

The most common visualization of SHAP Values is the beeswarm plot, which shows the impact of all variables across all samples:

python

```
shap.plots.beeswarm(shap_values)
```

This graph allows identifying:

- Which variables have the greatest global impact on predictions

- The average direction of that impact (positive or negative)

- The distribution of individual effects per feature

Another important visualization is the bar plot that summarizes feature importance based on the mean absolute value of SHAP Values:

python

```
shap.plots.bar(shap_values)
```

Unlike feature_importances_, which measures frequency or gain at splits, SHAP Values represent the actual impact of each variable on model decisions, based on its interactions with other features.

To analyze the local impact of a feature on a specific prediction, the waterfall plot is used:

python

```
shap.plots.waterfall(shap_values[0])
```

This plot shows how each variable contributed to the prediction of a single sample, clearly explaining why the model predicted a certain value for that input.

The difference between local and global explanations is central to the use of SHAP:

- Global explanations: indicate the model's average behavior and feature importance ranking

- Local explanations: analyze a specific prediction, detailing the individual influence of variables in that instance

These two dimensions are complementary. While global explanation helps understand the model as a whole, local explanation is vital for audits, justifications, and control of automated decisions at the individual level.

Another powerful resource is the dependence plot, which shows how a feature's value affects its impact on the model:

python

```
shap.plots.scatter(shap_values[:, "idade"], color=shap_values)
```

This graph allows identifying nonlinearities, interactions, and value ranges that amplify or reverse a variable's impact.

For practical applications, SHAP Values can be exported and integrated into dashboards with tools like Streamlit, Dash, Power BI, or custom web applications. The use of interactive charts with explanatory tooltips and segmentation by user groups enables the creation of interfaces that transparently explain model behavior.

In regulated environments, such as finance and healthcare, SHAP Values can be used as the basis for generating automated justification reports for decisions such as credit approvals, assisted diagnoses, or risk classification.

Another strategic use is drift analysis in production: by monitoring the SHAP Values of new predictions over time, it is possible to detect changes in model behavior or input data distribution, even without access to the true target value.

python

```
shap_mean = shap_values.values.mean(axis=0)
print(shap_mean)
```

By comparing the average SHAP values across different periods, it is possible to detect if the model has started relying more or less on certain variables, indicating a potential shift in data patterns.

Common Error Resolution

Error: ValueError: Model type not yet supported by SHAP
Cause: Model not trained with a structure compatible with shap.Explainer.

Solution: Ensure the model is of type XGBClassifier or XGBRegressor with numeric input.

Error: MemoryError when processing large volume of SHAP Values
Cause: Explainer created in exact mode with extensive data.
Solution: Use smaller samples or set approximate=True to save memory.

Error: Plot showing feature_names as f0, f1... without readable names
Cause: Model trained with NumPy array without named columns.
Solution: Train the model with pandas.DataFrame maintaining the original feature names.

Error: Dependence plot showing unexpected inverted pattern
Cause: Correlation with another higher-impact variable or undetected interaction.
Solution: Analyze conditional dependence between variables with interactive SHAP graphs.

Error: Waterfall plot error when accessing shap_values[i]
Cause: Direct access to the index without checking shap_values type.
Solution: Ensure shap_values is correctly indexed with shap_values[i].

Best Practices

- Use shap.Explainer directly on XGBoost models for full compatibility

- Generate beeswarm plots to identify features with the greatest global impact

- Apply waterfall plots to clearly justify individual decisions

- Use dependence plots to detect nonlinear effects and variable interactions

- Export SHAP Values for dashboards and automated audit or explanation reports

Strategic Summary

The interpretation of models with SHAP Values places XGBoost at a new level of transparency and reliability. The ability to decompose each model decision into understandable components strengthens machine learning system governance, facilitates stakeholder communication, and allows for systematic validation of internal logic. By combining local explanations, global analysis, and integration with visual interfaces, the use of SHAP transforms a high-performance model into an explainable, defensible, and sustainable decision-making tool in any technical or regulatory environment.

CHAPTER 17. SAVING AND LOADING MODELS

After training and validating an XGBoost model, ensuring that it can be reused with safety, portability, and version control is fundamental for the continuity of any machine learning pipeline. Correct model saving enables its application in production, integration with APIs, use in dashboard interfaces, or as part of embedded solutions. This chapter presents the safest and most efficient methods for saving and loading XGBoost models using pickle, joblib, and the library's native format, along with versioning practices and protection measures for corporate environments.

The simplest and most well-known method for persisting Python objects, including trained models, is using the pickle module. Although widely compatible, pickle has security limitations and portability issues between environment versions:

python

```python
import pickle


with open('modelo_xgb.pkl', 'wb') as f:
    pickle.dump(model, f)
```

To reload the saved model:

python

```
with open('modelo_xgb.pkl', 'rb') as f:
    modelo_carregado = pickle.load(f)
```

Joblib, also widely used in data science, is more efficient than pickle for large objects, such as models with many parameters, trees, or large-scale numeric data:

python

```
import joblib


joblib.dump(model, 'modelo_xgb.joblib')
modelo_carregado = joblib.load('modelo_xgb.joblib')
```

Both methods work well when the execution environment is controlled, that is, when the Python version, libraries, and operating system are compatible. For production environments or distribution across different machines, it is ideal to use XGBoost's native format, which is independent of language and version:

python

```
model.save_model('modelo_xgb.json')
```

To reload the model:

python

```
from xgboost import XGBClassifier


modelo_restaurado = XGBClassifier()
modelo_restaurado.load_model('modelo_xgb.json')
```

This format supports interoperability with libraries in R, Java, C++, and other languages compatible with XGBoost's structure, making it ideal for large-scale production and distributed systems.

For models based on Booster (lower-level format), the equivalent function is:

python

```
booster = model.get_booster()
booster.save_model('booster_xgb.bin')
```

And reloading:

python

```
import xgboost as xgb


booster_carregado = xgb.Booster()
booster_carregado.load_model('booster_xgb.bin')
```

Using the .json or .bin format is highly recommended when the model needs to be decoupled from the Python environment or integrated into external systems. It also allows manual inspection, auditing, and compatibility with visualization tools.

In collaborative projects or versioned systems, it is essential to adopt model versioning practices, recording metadata such as:

- Training date and time

- Source dataset

- Library and Python versions

- Parameters used

- Performance metrics on the validation set

These details can be saved in a .txt, .yaml, .json file or incorporated into the model file name:

python

```python
metadados = {
    'modelo': 'xgb_classificador',
    'data_treinamento': '2025-04-25',
    'dataset': 'clientes.csv',
    'metricas': {'AUC': 0.92, 'F1': 0.88},
    'versao_python': '3.9',
    'versao_xgboost': xgb.__version__
}


import json
with open('modelo_xgb_metadados.json', 'w') as f:
    json.dump(metadados, f, indent=4)
```

This practice prevents loss of context, facilitates reprocessing, and enables tracking which model was used in each situation.

For security and portability, it is recommended to:

- Not use pickle to load unknown files from external sources.

- Verify hashes or signatures of received files.

- Document environment versions with pip freeze or conda env export.

- Use Docker containers with frozen environments for greater reliability.

- Include automated tests to verify that the loaded model generates consistent predictions.

In production pipelines with APIs, it is common to load the model at the server startup using Flask, FastAPI, or Django:

python

```
# fastapi_app.py
from fastapi import FastAPI
import joblib


app = FastAPI()
model = joblib.load('modelo_xgb.joblib')


@app.post("/prever")
def prever(dados: dict):
    X = pd.DataFrame([dados])
    y_pred = model.predict(X)
    return {"classe": int(y_pred[0])}
```

Another common pattern is saving the model in centralized repositories such as Amazon S3, Google Cloud Storage, MLflow, or DVC (Data Version Control). This allows managing multiple model versions, integrating with CI/CD, and automating deploy processes.

Common Error Resolution

Error: AttributeError: Can't get attribute 'XGBClassifier' on <module 'main'>
Cause: Model saved with pickle and reloaded in a different context.
Solution: Ensure the loading script has the same imports as the original environment.

Error: XGBoostError: [15:15:48] .../learner.cc:836: Check failed
Cause: Attempt to load a model saved with an incompatible XGBoost version.
Solution: Verify and align library versions between environments.

Error: TypeError: Object of type Booster is not JSON serializable
Cause: Attempt to save the object with json.dump().
Solution: Use booster.save_model() for proper persistence.

Error: ValueError when predicting after loading the model
Cause: Change in feature structure between training and prediction.
Solution: Save and restore column names and order along with the model.

Error: ModuleNotFoundError when loading with joblib
Cause: Execution environment without the same package structure.
Solution: Use virtualenvs and requirements files to replicate the environment.

Best Practices

- Prefer model.save_model() for greater portability and

security

- Save technical metadata along with the model file

- Test the loaded model with real samples before using it in production

- Control environment versions with pip freeze and requirements.txt

- Include signature or hash in model files in sensitive environments

Strategic Summary

Saving and loading models with XGBoost is a critical point of integration between development and production application. Choosing the correct format, controlling the environment, and ensuring portability and security are essential practices to maintain the reliability of predictive solutions at scale. By mastering these processes, the professional ensures that the value generated during model training is preserved, auditable, and applicable across multiple operational scenarios.

CHAPTER 18. INTEGRATION WITH FLASK AND FASTAPI

Turning an XGBoost model into a predictive API is an essential step to allow web applications, corporate systems, or external devices to send data and receive predictions in real time. The Flask and FastAPI libraries offer efficient and robust paths for this integration, enabling local, cloud, or Docker-encapsulated deployment. This chapter presents the construction of predictive APIs with Flask and FastAPI, from basic structure to functional deployment, including testing practices and endpoint operation control.

Creating an API with Flask starts from the idea of turning the prediction function into an HTTP endpoint, which receives data in JSON format, processes it, and returns the response to the client. After training and saving the model with joblib, the API can be structured as follows:

python

```
# app_flask.py
from flask import Flask, request, jsonify
import joblib
import pandas as pd


app = Flask(__name__)
model = joblib.load('modelo_xgb.joblib')
```

```python
@app.route('/prever', methods=['POST'])
def prever():
    dados = request.get_json()
    X = pd.DataFrame([dados])
    y_pred = model.predict(X)
    return jsonify({'classe': int(y_pred[0])})


if __name__ == '__main__':
    app.run(debug=True, host='0.0.0.0', port=5000)
```

With the server running, the endpoint can be tested with tools like Postman, Curl, or Python scripts:

bash

```bash
curl -X POST http://localhost:5000/prever -H "Content-Type: application/json" -d '{"idade": 35, "salario": 4200, "tempo_de_empresa": 3}'
```

FastAPI offers a modern and high-performance alternative, with native support for automatic documentation, data validation via pydantic, and optimized performance with uvicorn. The same model can be exposed with FastAPI as follows:

python

```python
# app_fastapi.py
from fastapi import FastAPI
from pydantic import BaseModel
```

```
import joblib
import pandas as pd

class Entrada(BaseModel):
    idade: int
    salario: float
    tempo_de_empresa: int

app = FastAPI()
model = joblib.load('modelo_xgb.joblib')

@app.post("/prever")
def prever(dados: Entrada):
    X = pd.DataFrame([dados.dict()])
    y_pred = model.predict(X)
    return {"classe": int(y_pred[0])}
```

To run the application:

bash

```
uvicorn app_fastapi:app --reload --host 0.0.0.0 --port 8000
```

FastAPI automatically generates the Swagger interface at the / docs route, facilitating direct testing without external tools. This is especially useful for validation and collaborative documentation.

Local deployment ensures the application works in the development environment, but deploying via Docker ensures portability, scalability, and full control over the environment. The Dockerfile for both APIs follows a simple structure:

dockerfile

```
FROM python:3.9


WORKDIR /app
COPY . /app


RUN pip install -r requirements.txt


CMD ["uvicorn", "app_fastapi:app", "--host", "0.0.0.0", "--port", "8000"]
```

The requirements.txt should contain all project dependencies, such as:

nginx

```
nginx

fastapi

uvicorn

joblib

pandas

xgboost

scikit-learn
```

To build and run the container:

bash

```bash
docker build -t xgb-api .
docker run -p 8000:8000 xgb-api
```

Using Docker allows replicating the environment exactly on other machines or cloud servers, eliminating compatibility problems.

To ensure that endpoints are operational, it is recommended to create automated tests using pytest, requests, or continuous integration tools:

python

```python
import requests

url = "http://localhost:8000/prever"
dados = {"idade": 45, "salario": 3500.0, "tempo_de_empresa": 5}

resposta = requests.post(url, json=dados)
print(resposta.json())
```

These tests can be included in CI/CD routines to automatically validate the API's stability whenever the code is changed or updated.

During model integration with the API, it is essential to ensure that the structure of the received data matches the data used during training, preserving column order and types. Any change, such as a change in category encoding, can compromise prediction.

It is also possible to add security with basic authentication, request limits, or integration with OAuth2 authentication and JWT tokens when the API is publicly exposed.

Common Error Resolution

Error: ValueError: Number of features of the model does not match input
Cause: Difference in input structure between the trained model and the API data.
Solution: Ensure that the DataFrame received in the API has columns in the same order and format.

Error: JSONDecodeError when receiving the request
Cause: Payload sent malformed or not recognized as JSON.
Solution: Validate the request body and use application/json in the header.

Error: ModuleNotFoundError in Docker container
Cause: Missing libraries in requirements.txt.
Solution: Review dependencies and rebuild Docker image.

Error: 422 Unprocessable Entity error in FastAPI
Cause: Data sent does not match the types defined in pydantic.
Solution: Ensure that the types (int, float, string) are correct in the request body.

Error: API works locally but fails when exposed publicly
Cause: Firewall restrictions or incorrect host bindings.
Solution: Use 0.0.0.0 as host and configure the network environment correctly.

Best Practices

- Define pydantic models for strict input validation in

FastAPI

- Expose only necessary endpoints and apply authentication for public environments

- Use Docker to encapsulate the API and the model with full version control

- Include automated tests with real calls to the endpoint to ensure stability

- Log requests and responses for auditing and monitoring

Strategic Summary

Integrating an XGBoost model with Flask or FastAPI greatly expands its reach and applicability, transforming a data artifact into a service ready for consumption by any system. With simple, efficient, and secure structures, it is possible to operationalize real-time predictions, offer scalable APIs via Docker, and maintain full traceability and control of the environment. This capability is essential to applying artificial intelligence with direct impact on organizational processes and decisions.

CHAPTER 19. INTEGRATION WITH STREAMLIT

Transforming an XGBoost model into an interactive application with an accessible visual interface is a powerful way to deliver value directly to the end user. The Streamlit library allows building dashboards and graphical interfaces for machine learning with just a few lines of code, without the need for complex front-end frameworks. With interactive components, real-time data input support, and simplified deployment, Streamlit is the ideal solution for presenting trained models with clarity, customization, and functionality. This chapter presents the construction of predictive interfaces with Streamlit, from the basic structure to strategies for sharing and deployment.

After training and saving the model with joblib, creating an application with Streamlit starts by building an interface in a single Python script. Below is an example of a classification application using XGBoost:

python

```python
# app_streamlit.py
import streamlit as st
import joblib
import pandas as pd


# Load the trained model
```

```python
model = joblib.load('modelo_xgb.joblib')


# Application title
st.title("XGBoost Classifier - Risk Prediction")


# Collect user inputs
age = st.slider("Age", 18, 100, 30)
salary = st.number_input("Salary", min_value=1000.0,
value=4000.0)
years_at_company = st.slider("Years at Company", 0, 40, 5)


# Create input DataFrame
input_data = pd.DataFrame([[age, salary, years_at_company]],
                columns=['idade', 'salario',
'tempo_de_empresa'])


# Predict and display the result
if st.button("Predict"):
    prediction = model.predict(input_data)
    st.write(f"Predicted class: {int(prediction[0])}")
```

This code generates a responsive interface with sliders, input fields, and an action button. The application is launched using:

bash

```bash
streamlit run app_streamlit.py
```

At every user interaction, the values are automatically updated and the model returns a prediction based on the provided inputs.

The main interactive components of Streamlit include:

- st.slider(): **numeric range selection**

- st.number_input(): **direct number input**

- st.text_input(): **text input**

- st.selectbox() and st.radio(): **category selection**

- st.file_uploader(): **uploading files like CSV, Excel, or images**

- st.button(): **triggers actions and events**

These components can be combined to simulate real-world forms, recommendation systems, risk assessments, and other interactive applications based on predictions.

It is possible to customize the layout by using columns, sidebars, and separators:

python

```
with st.sidebar:
    age = st.slider("Age", 18, 100, 30)
    salary = st.number_input("Salary", min_value=1000.0,
value=4000.0)
    years_at_company = st.slider("Years at Company", 0, 40, 5)
```

This feature helps to visually organize the application, especially when dealing with many input variables.

In addition to predictions, you can display charts, tables, and formatted texts using:

- st.line_chart(), st.bar_chart(), st.area_chart()

- st.dataframe() and st.table()

- st.markdown() for formatted text

- st.plotly_chart() and st.pyplot() for integrating with visualization libraries

These elements allow incorporating exploratory analysis, result comparisons, and model explanations in a visual and intuitive manner.

The application can be deployed locally, on a private server, on cloud instances, or directly on Streamlit Cloud, which offers free hosting for GitHub repositories. To deploy:

- Have a public repository with the app.py script

- Add a requirements.txt with the necessary dependencies:

nginx

nginx

streamlit

pandas

joblib

xgboost

scikit-learn

- Publish the repository and connect it to Streamlit Cloud

- Click "New App", select the repository, and define the main script

Deployment is automatic and the generated link can be shared with anyone.

Another option is to embed the Streamlit app into a Docker container for corporate or internal deployments:

dockerfile

```
FROM python:3.9

WORKDIR /app
COPY . /app

RUN pip install -r requirements.txt

CMD ["streamlit", "run", "app_streamlit.py", "--server.port=8501", "--server.enableCORS=false"]
```

This format enables version control, scalability, and integration with orchestrators such as Docker Compose and Kubernetes.

During the use of the interface, it is crucial to maintain compatibility between user inputs and the model's expected input format. Any inconsistency in names, order, or data types can cause prediction errors. To ensure stability, always validate the received data:

python

```
try:
    prediction = model.predict(input_data)
    st.success(f"Predicted class: {int(prediction[0])}")
except Exception as e:
    st.error(f"Prediction error: {e}")
```

Moreover, for systems that use files as input, it is possible to upload and process them directly:

python

```
file = st.file_uploader("Upload CSV for batch prediction",
type="csv")

if file is not None:
    data = pd.read_csv(file)
    predictions = model.predict(data)
    st.write("Results:")
    st.dataframe(pd.DataFrame(predictions,
columns=['Predicted Class']))
```

This functionality expands the interface's usage for operational teams who wish to predict multiple records without needing to resort to scripts or APIs.

Common Error Resolution

Error: ValueError: Number of features of the model does not match input

Cause: Difference in order or columns between inputs.
Solution: Ensure consistency of names, types, and order of columns with the training data.

Error: Streamlit does not recognize the button or event does not fire
Cause: Lack of indentation or incorrect scope inside if st.button().
Solution: Maintain correct structure and avoid placing inputs outside the button's scope.

Error: No module named 'streamlit'
Cause: Streamlit library not installed.
Solution: Install using pip install streamlit or add it to requirements.txt.

Error: UnicodeDecodeError when reading uploaded CSV
Cause: File encoding incompatible with UTF-8.
Solution: Try pd.read_csv(file, encoding='latin1') or display a controlled error message.

Error: Slow interface with large data volumes
Cause: Non-optimized processing or displaying too many rows.
Solution: Restrict the number of displayed records and optimize preprocessing.

Best Practices

- Validate input data before sending to the model

- Use sidebars to organize variables and control options

- Show success, error, and loading messages for a smooth user experience

- Deploy the model with Streamlit Cloud or Docker for controlled access

- Ensure the code remains clean, modular, and maintainable

Strategic Summary

Integrating XGBoost models with Streamlit allows delivering intelligence in an interactive, clear, and actionable way. With a few commands and no front-end dependencies, it is possible to create professional-grade interfaces that expose the model's value with accessibility and practicality. This approach shortens the path between development and real-world application, placing the model in the hands of both technical and non-technical users, promoting data-driven decisions with simplicity and precision.

CHAPTER 20. XGBOOST WITH GPU

Using GPU to accelerate XGBoost model training represents a significant advance in the computational efficiency of machine learning pipelines. With native support for NVIDIA's CUDA architecture, XGBoost can drastically reduce training times, especially on large datasets with high dimensionality. However, adopting GPU requires specific installation, compatibility verification, and benchmarking practices to measure the real performance gains. This chapter presents the installation of XGBoost with CUDA support, comparative execution with CPU, the main system requirements, and recommendations to fully leverage GPU acceleration.

To use GPU with XGBoost, it is necessary to install a version compiled with CUDA support. This installation can be done via conda-forge, provided that the environment has a CUDA Toolkit compatible with the machine's GPU:

bash

```
conda install -c nvidia -c rapidsai -c conda-forge \
    xgboost cudatoolkit=11.2
```

Another way to ensure proper installation is to compile XGBoost from the source code with explicit CUDA support. This process is more technical and recommended only when no prebuilt binaries are available for your system version.

To verify if GPU installation was successful, you can train a

model with the parameter tree_method='gpu_hist':

python

```
from xgboost import XGBClassifier


modelo_gpu = XGBClassifier(
    tree_method='gpu_hist',
    predictor='gpu_predictor',
    use_label_encoder=False,
    eval_metric='logloss'
)
modelo_gpu.fit(X_train, y_train)
```

If execution proceeds without error, the GPU has been recognized and is being utilized. The gpu_hist method is the fastest available and replaces the traditional CPU hist algorithm with a version optimized for parallel execution on the GPU.

To compare performance between CPU and GPU, training can be performed in both modes while measuring the execution time:

python

```
import time
from xgboost import XGBClassifier


# Training on CPU
modelo_cpu = XGBClassifier(
    tree_method='hist',
    use_label_encoder=False,
```

```
    eval_metric='logloss'
)

start_cpu = time.time()
modelo_cpu.fit(X_train, y_train)
end_cpu = time.time()
print(f"CPU Time: {end_cpu - start_cpu:.2f} seconds")

# Training on GPU
modelo_gpu = XGBClassifier(
    tree_method='gpu_hist',
    predictor='gpu_predictor',
    use_label_encoder=False,
    eval_metric='logloss'
)

start_gpu = time.time()
modelo_gpu.fit(X_train, y_train)
end_gpu = time.time()
print(f"GPU Time: {end_gpu - start_gpu:.2f} seconds")
```

The time difference can be significant on larger datasets. Generally, the GPU offers substantial gains when the number of instances exceeds 100,000 records or when there are many predictor variables.

It is important to verify GPU compatibility with the CUDA

Toolkit version used during installation. The command nvidia-smi displays the GPU specifications and the installed driver version. The CUDA version used by XGBoost must be compatible with the NVIDIA driver version.

bash

```
nvidia-smi
```

Moreover, the cudatoolkit package installed via conda must match the capabilities of the GPU. Installing versions higher than what the GPU supports may cause silent failures or execution in CPU mode even with gpu_hist specified.

Another important point is using predictor='gpu_predictor', which ensures that both training and inference are executed on the GPU. Using only tree_method='gpu_hist' may result in training on the GPU but prediction falling back to the CPU if not properly specified.

When using GPU on shared servers, clusters, or remote notebooks, it is necessary to ensure that the GPU is free. In some environments, multiple tasks compete for the same resource, reducing performance gains. Tools like nvidia-smi and gpustat help monitor real-time GPU usage.

In cases of multiple GPUs, XGBoost does not yet natively utilize all cards in parallel. To leverage multiple GPUs, data partitioning and parallel training must be performed manually, or frameworks like Dask or Spark should be used for distributed processing.

Common Error Resolution

Error: XGBoostError: GPU support is not enabled
Cause: XGBoost installation without CUDA support.
Solution: Reinstall via conda with cudatoolkit, or compile with

GPU enabled.

Error: CUDA driver version is insufficient for CUDA runtime
Cause: Outdated or incompatible NVIDIA driver.
Solution: Update the driver to a version compatible with the installed cudatoolkit.

Error: RuntimeError: No GPU device found
Cause: No GPU detected or GPU disabled.
Solution: Verify with nvidia-smi and ensure GPU availability.

Error: Prediction done on CPU even with GPU activated
Cause: Missing predictor='gpu_predictor' parameter.
Solution: Specify the predictor parameter to maintain inference on GPU.

Error: Very small model with no noticeable performance gain
Cause: Lightweight dataset does not justify GPU use.
Solution: Use GPU only when the data volume warrants acceleration.

Best Practices

- Use tree_method='gpu_hist' and predictor='gpu_predictor' together

- Verify compatibility between GPU, driver, and CUDA Toolkit version

- Benchmark real performance gains before integrating GPU into the pipeline

- Monitor GPU usage with nvidia-smi during training

- Fallback to CPU in environments where GPU offers no significant advantage

Strategic Summary

Using XGBoost with GPU is one of the most direct ways to scale machine learning projects efficiently, reducing execution times without changing model logic. With proper configuration, it is possible to train robust models in seconds, optimizing development cycles and deployment in production environments. Understanding technical dependencies, measuring real gains, and adopting safe execution practices ensure that GPU acceleration adds value without compromising the solution's stability.

CHAPTER 21. PERFORMANCE EVALUATION WITH DASK

XGBoost can be integrated with Dask to leverage parallelization and task distribution across multiple cores or machines. This approach is useful for large-scale datasets that exceed available RAM, or when it is necessary to reduce model training time without sacrificing performance. Dask enables XGBoost models to be trained in a distributed manner on local clusters or in cloud computing environments, while maintaining compatibility with the Python ecosystem. This chapter presents how to run XGBoost with Dask, configure a local cluster for testing, and perform scalability analysis to validate actual performance gains.

To use Dask with XGBoost, it is necessary to install the compatible packages:

bash

```
pip install dask[complete] dask-xgboost xgboost dask-ml
```

The first step is to configure a local cluster with multiple workers. This can be done directly within the code:

python

```
from dask.distributed import Client, LocalCluster

cluster = LocalCluster(n_workers=4, threads_per_worker=1)
```

```
client = Client(cluster)
```

The LocalCluster creates a parallel execution environment on a single machine, using multiple cores. It is ideal for testing before scaling to remote clusters.

With the client active, the next step is to prepare the data with Dask:

python

```
import dask.dataframe as dd

import dask.array as da

from sklearn.datasets import make_classification


# Generate synthetic data

X_np, y_np = make_classification(n_samples=100000, n_features=50, random_state=42)


# Convert to Dask Array

X = da.from_array(X_np, chunks=(10000, -1))

y = da.from_array(y_np, chunks=(10000,))
```

The Dask interface allows you to work with arrays and dataframes that behave like traditional NumPy and Pandas objects but with distributed chunk processing.

To train XGBoost with Dask, use xgboost.dask:

python

```
import xgboost as xgb
```

```
dtrain = xgb.dask.DaskDMatrix(client, X, y)

params = {
    'objective': 'binary:logistic',
    'max_depth': 6,
    'eta': 0.1,
    'subsample': 0.8,
    'eval_metric': 'auc'
}

output = xgb.dask.train(client, params, dtrain,
num_boost_round=100)
booster = output['booster']
```

This process distributes the training across the cluster's workers. The resulting booster object is compatible with traditional XGBoost and can be saved, loaded, or used for predictions.

Prediction is also done in a distributed way:

python

```
y_pred = xgb.dask.predict(client, booster, X)
print(y_pred.compute())
```

Since y_pred is a Dask Array, it is necessary to call .compute() to materialize the result into memory.

Scalability analysis can be done by monitoring execution time with different configurations of n_workers and threads_per_worker. The Dask dashboard can be accessed via browser to visualize CPU usage, memory, throughput, and task latency:

python

client

Distributed execution tends to bring greater benefit in:

- Datasets with millions of rows

- Datasets with many features

- Environments with multiple cores or parallel instances

- Repetitive processes like tuning with cross-validation

To evaluate real performance gains, training time with Dask is compared to training time with traditional XGBoost. The reduction in time, combined with maintenance of the main accuracy or metric, indicates scalability success.

Besides LocalCluster, Dask can also be used with:

- SSHCluster for multiple machines on the network

- KubeCluster in Kubernetes environments

- EC2Cluster or GCPCluster on cloud providers

- Dask Gateway for authentication control in multi-user environments

These modes allow horizontal scaling of training, ideal for teams operating large data volumes with distributed computational resources.

Common Error Resolution

Error: ImportError: No module named 'dask_xgboost'
Cause: Package not installed correctly or incompatible version.
Solution: Install with pip install dask-xgboost and verify compatibility with xgboost.

Error: ValueError: Cannot convert Dask object to numpy array
Cause: Attempt to use X.values without computing the Dask Array.
Solution: Use X.compute() only when necessary or keep it as a Dask Array.

Error: Timeout when starting cluster
Cause: Insufficient CPU or RAM resource or port conflict.
Solution: Reduce n_workers, restart the kernel, or free system ports.

Error: Worse performance with Dask than with local execution
Cause: Small dataset or unnecessary parallelization overhead.
Solution: Use Dask only when the parallelization cost is justified.

Error: Client unexpectedly closed
Cause: Communication failure with the cluster or aborted process.
Solution: Check logs, update packages, and restart the execution environment.

Best Practices

- Use appropriate chunks based on available memory

- Monitor the Dask dashboard to understand bottlenecks

- Validate model consistency with metrics after parallelization

- Compare execution times to justify cluster use

- Apply .persist() or .compute() with control to avoid memory overflows

Strategic Summary

The integration between XGBoost and Dask enables scaling model training beyond the memory and CPU limits of a single machine. With simple tools and compatibility with familiar structures, it is possible to distribute processing, reduce execution times, and prepare high-performance pipelines for production. Mastery of this approach positions the professional to operate in massive data environments with technical robustness and optimized infrastructure to deliver predictive models at real scale.

CHAPTER 22. XGBOOST ON AWS SAGEMAKER

Amazon SageMaker is a managed service for developing, training, deploying, and monitoring machine learning models at scale. By integrating XGBoost with SageMaker, it is possible to automate much of the model lifecycle, from data upload to production deployment with a REST endpoint, using scalable infrastructure integrated with other AWS services. This chapter presents the practical use of XGBoost within SageMaker, focusing on data preparation, creation of inference endpoints, and operational monitoring strategies.

Using XGBoost on SageMaker can be done either with custom scripts in containers or with the precompiled algorithm provided by AWS, optimized for performance on cloud infrastructure. The most direct approach uses the integrated estimator sagemaker.xgboost.estimator.XGBoost.

Before training, it is necessary to upload the data to Amazon S3. SageMaker uses S3 buckets as a data source for both training and validation and for deployment:

python

```
import sagemaker
from sagemaker import Session
import boto3


sess = sagemaker.Session()
```

```python
bucket = sess.default_bucket()

prefix = 'xgboost-project'


s3_input_path = sess.upload_data(path='data/train.csv',
bucket=bucket, key_prefix=f'{prefix}/input')
```

With the data available in S3, the XGBoost estimator is created using AWS's official container:

python

```python
from sagemaker.inputs import TrainingInput

from sagemaker.xgboost.estimator import XGBoost


xgb_estimator = XGBoost(
    entry_point='train.py',
    framework_version='1.3-1',
    hyperparameters={
        'max_depth': 5,
        'eta': 0.2,
        'objective': 'binary:logistic',
        'num_round': 100
    },
    role=sagemaker.get_execution_role(),
    instance_count=1,
    instance_type='ml.m5.xlarge',
    output_path=f's3://{bucket}/{prefix}/output'
```

```
)

train_input = TrainingInput(s3_data=s3_input_path,
content_type='csv')

xgb_estimator.fit({'train': train_input})
```

The train.py script must follow the standard SageMaker interface, receiving arguments via argparse and saving the model in the /opt/ml/model folder. AWS manages the environment, isolates dependencies, and packages the trained model.

With the model ready, a REST endpoint can be created with just one line of code:

python

```
predictor = xgb_estimator.deploy(

    initial_instance_count=1,

    instance_type='ml.m5.large'

)
```

This endpoint can be called via HTTP with JSON or CSV payloads, depending on the input configuration. Inference is performed with low latency and automatic scalability:

python

```
response = predictor.predict(data)

print(response)
```

SageMaker also allows versioning of endpoints, creating backup models, and performing blue/green deployment, where two models can run in parallel for comparative evaluation before replacing the main model.

Monitoring the model in production is handled by SageMaker Model Monitor, which collects inference metrics, detects input data drift, compares prediction distributions, and alerts for anomalous behaviors. This service can be activated with a few commands:

python

```python
from sagemaker.model_monitor import DataCaptureConfig


data_capture_config = DataCaptureConfig(
    enable_capture=True,
    sampling_percentage=100,
    destination_s3_uri=f's3://{bucket}/{prefix}/monitor'
)


predictor = xgb_estimator.deploy(
    initial_instance_count=1,
    instance_type='ml.m5.large',
    data_capture_config=data_capture_config
)
```

The metrics are integrated with Amazon CloudWatch, allowing graphical visualization, alarm setting, and integration with automated response pipelines.

Common Error Resolution

Error: ClientError: AccessDenied
Cause: Inadequate permission to write to the S3 bucket.
Solution: Check the execution role's policy for SageMaker.

Error: TrainingJobError: Algorithm error
Cause: Data structure incompatible with the expected format.
Solution: Ensure correct encoding and remove headers or non-numeric columns.

Error: Endpoint timed out
Cause: Heavy model running on an instance with insufficient resources.
Solution: Use instances with more memory or reduce model complexity.

Error: MissingModelError when creating endpoint
Cause: Output directory without a saved model.
Solution: Ensure train.py saves the artifact correctly to /opt/ml/model.

Error: Unrecognized input content-type
Cause: Payload incompatible with the configured endpoint type.
Solution: Adjust request headers or use predictor.serializer = CSVSerializer().

Best Practices

- Validate scripts locally before uploading to SageMaker

- Use separate buckets for input, output, and monitoring logs

- Set thresholds and alarms in CloudWatch for anomalous events

- Version training code and models with timestamps and metadata

- Document parameterization decisions for reproducibility

Strategic Summary

Using XGBoost within AWS SageMaker simplifies the deployment of models into production with scalable infrastructure, automated monitoring, and direct integration with the cloud ecosystem. By consolidating training, deployment, and post-model analysis into a single managed environment, data professionals gain agility, security, and control. Mastery of these tools, combined with a thorough understanding of inference and monitoring processes, positions XGBoost not only as an efficient algorithm but as a core component of robust and operational predictive solutions.

CHAPTER 23. MODELING IN ENTERPRISE PROJECTS

Modeling with XGBoost in enterprise environments requires more than technical mastery of the library. It demands understanding business requirements, aligning expectations among multidisciplinary teams, and operating within formal validation, deployment, and monitoring cycles. Modeling in corporate contexts involves integration with legacy systems, regulatory concerns, data governance, and commitments to reproducible and auditable deliveries. This chapter presents how to structure the use of XGBoost in enterprise projects, from gathering requirements to integrated operation with technical, analytical, and executive teams.

The starting point for enterprise projects with XGBoost is a clear understanding of business requirements. These requirements define technical constraints, success metrics, model usage frequency, and direct operational impacts on the organization. Common examples include:

- Credit risk classification for automated approval

- Churn prediction for customer retention

- Lead classification for sales prioritization

- Demand forecasting for inventory control

- Anomaly detection in financial transactions

Each case demands not only predictive performance but also interpretability, traceability, and operational stability. The evaluation metric should not be defined solely by the technical team but in collaboration with business stakeholders, considering real impacts such as error cost, revenue impact, and legal requirements.

The lifecycle of an XGBoost model in an enterprise context involves multiple stages beyond training and testing:

- Requirement gathering

- Data engineering and feature definition

- Initial training and validation

- Hyperparameter tuning with cross-validation

- Validation with stakeholders and internal committees

- Controlled deployment (AB testing, shadow mode, or pilot)

- Continuous monitoring with logging and metrics

- Scheduled updating with versioning

This cycle can last from weeks to months, depending on the model's criticality. It is common for models to undergo multiple revisions before being considered ready for production.

XGBoost facilitates this process with:

- Robust performance on structured data

- Compatibility with APIs via Flask/FastAPI

- Export to lightweight and portable formats (JSON, binary)

- Integration with tools such as MLflow, DVC, and Airflow

- Interpretability with SHAP, enabling explanations for internal audits

A central point of enterprise modeling is the integration between teams. A successful project involves:

- Data engineers: responsible for ETL pipelines and provisioning variables

- Data scientists: responsible for modeling, tuning, and validation

- Machine learning engineers: responsible for deployment, monitoring, and operational performance

- Product Owners and business analysts: responsible for translating company objectives into acceptance criteria and feasibility

Communication among these actors must be continuous and clear, with intermediate deliverables and regular checkpoints. Model documentation, both technical and functional, must be updated at each iteration.

For system integration, XGBoost models are generally served as REST APIs, incorporated into microservices, or executed in batch mode. The choice depends on usage frequency:

- Real-time: APIs with instant return, used in flows such as customer scoring, order validation, or fraud monitoring.

- Near real-time: processing in minute-level windows with data buffering.

- Batch: daily, weekly, or monthly execution, common in reporting, forecasting, and audits.

The model version, file hash, input data structure, and hyperparameter configuration must be recorded with each release. This ensures reproducibility, auditability, and rollback capability in case of failures.

Common Error Resolution

Error: Model approved in testing but fails in production
Cause: Difference between training data and operational data.
Solution: Ensure the production pipeline mirrors the training pipeline, including preprocessing steps.

Error: Stakeholders do not trust predictions
Cause: Lack of interpretability or poorly presented explanations.
Solution: Use SHAP Values and dashboards focused on impact and decision justification.

Error: Model performs well initially and degrades over time
Cause: Data drift or market behavior change.
Solution: Continuously monitor performance metrics and implement retraining strategies.

Error: Deployment interrupted by dependency problems
Cause: Production environment with different libraries than training environment.
Solution: Use containers (Docker) or controlled virtualenvs with requirements.txt files.

Error: Runtime error due to malformed input
Cause: API receiving inputs in a format different from what the model expects.
Solution: Apply schema validation using Pydantic or JSON Schema at the input layer.

Best Practices

- Collect business metrics before starting modeling

- Maintain living and accessible documentation throughout the project

- Separate training, testing, and production environments with versioning

- Test models with real data before official deployment

- Establish retraining processes with automatic checkpoints and alerts

Strategic Summary

Applying XGBoost in enterprise projects demands more than accuracy: it requires a deep understanding of business objectives, collaboration between departments, and solid operational architecture. By following a structured lifecycle, ensuring team integration, and maintaining best practices in versioning and documentation, it is possible to turn models into real organizational assets. XGBoost, for its versatility and compatibility, is a powerful technical choice to deliver operational intelligence with traceability, speed, and measurable strategic impact.

CHAPTER 24. CASE STUDIES WITH PUBLIC DATA

Applying XGBoost to public datasets is an important step for validating acquired knowledge, testing different modeling approaches, and understanding how the algorithm behaves in real-world contexts, with noise, collinearity, and diverse patterns. Working with widely known datasets also allows comparing results, interpreting metrics in a contextualized manner, and creating consistent technical references. This chapter presents case studies using public data from the Kaggle platform and the UCI Machine Learning Repository, focusing on performance analysis, modeling decisions, and interpretation of results obtained with XGBoost.

The first application uses the dataset "Titanic: Machine Learning from Disaster," one of the most famous introductory problems on Kaggle. The goal is to predict which passengers survived the shipwreck based on variables such as age, sex, class, fare, and number of companions.

After loading the dataset, a robust feature engineering step is necessary:

python

```
import pandas as pd


df = pd.read_csv('train.csv')
```

```python
df['Sex'] = df['Sex'].map({'male': 0, 'female': 1})
df['Embarked'].fillna('S', inplace=True)
df['Embarked'] = df['Embarked'].map({'S': 0, 'C': 1, 'Q': 2})
df['Age'].fillna(df['Age'].median(), inplace=True)
df['Fare'].fillna(df['Fare'].median(), inplace=True)
```

The target variable is Survived, and the predictors are selected based on exploratory analysis:

python

```python
features = ['Pclass', 'Sex', 'Age', 'SibSp', 'Parch', 'Fare', 'Embarked']
X = df[features]
y = df['Survived']
```

With the data ready, the model is trained with stratified cross-validation:

python

```python
from xgboost import XGBClassifier
from sklearn.model_selection import StratifiedKFold, cross_val_score


model = XGBClassifier(use_label_encoder=False, eval_metric='logloss')
kfold = StratifiedKFold(n_splits=5, shuffle=True, random_state=42)
scores = cross_val_score(model, X, y, scoring='accuracy',
```

```
cv=kfold)

print("Mean Accuracy:", scores.mean())
```

The performance obtained with XGBoost surpasses traditional linear models and allows exploring additional strategies such as imputation methods, derived feature creation, and hyperparameter tuning with GridSearchCV or RandomizedSearchCV.

The second case study uses the "Adult" dataset from UCI, aimed at predicting annual income based on demographic variables. The objective is to classify whether an individual earns more or less than 50,000 dollars per year, using attributes like age, education, occupation, and weekly working hours.

After loading, categorical data are encoded with LabelEncoder and missing values are treated by selective imputation or removal:

python

```
from sklearn.preprocessing import LabelEncoder

df = pd.read_csv('adult.csv', na_values='?')
df.dropna(inplace=True)

for col in df.select_dtypes(include='object'):
    df[col] = LabelEncoder().fit_transform(df[col])
```

Training and testing split is performed with train_test_split:

python

```
from sklearn.model_selection import train_test_split

X = df.drop('income', axis=1)
y = df['income']
X_train, X_test, y_train, y_test = train_test_split(X, y,
test_size=0.2, random_state=42)
```

The model is trained with parameter adjustment and evaluated by AUC:

python

```
from sklearn.metrics import roc_auc_score

model = XGBClassifier(n_estimators=150, max_depth=5,
learning_rate=0.1, use_label_encoder=False,
eval_metric='logloss')
model.fit(X_train, y_train)
y_proba = model.predict_proba(X_test)[:, 1]


print("AUC:", roc_auc_score(y_test, y_proba))
```

The analysis of SHAP Values on the test set reveals the impact of variables such as education_num, hours_per_week, and marital_status on the final prediction, strengthening model interpretability.

These case studies illustrate how the technical application of XGBoost directly connects to real-world problems, requiring structured decisions in preprocessing, metric choice, validation, and input data control.

Common Error Resolution

Error: ValueError when training with categorical columns
Cause: Data not converted to numeric before fitting.
Solution: Apply LabelEncoder, OneHotEncoder, or map() to transform categories.

Error: Inconsistent accuracy between training and validation
Cause: Overfitting due to excessive depth or lack of regularization.
Solution: Adjust max_depth, reduce learning_rate, use early_stopping_rounds.

Error: Irrelevant metrics for the problem's objective
Cause: Use of accuracy in imbalanced datasets.
Solution: Prioritize roc_auc, f1_score, or recall depending on the context.

Error: Model with high variation between folds
Cause: Imbalanced data or inadequate segmentation.
Solution: Use StratifiedKFold to maintain the target class proportion.

Error: Final result difficult to interpret for stakeholders
Cause: Lack of feature importance analysis or absence of explanations.
Solution: Integrate SHAP and explanatory visualizations with matplotlib or plotly.

Best Practices

- Validate all preprocessing steps with real data

- Use stratified cross-validation with multiple metrics

- Document modeling and parameterization decisions

- Include feature importance analysis and local explanations

- Test with widely used datasets for performance benchmarking

Strategic Summary

Case studies with public data are concrete opportunities to evaluate XGBoost in realistic scenarios and measure its ability to generate effective, interpretable, and applicable models. Working with datasets like Titanic and Adult strengthens the technical foundation, provides benchmarking references, and develops the ability to make structured decisions under practical pressure. This experience brings supervised modeling closer to operational reality, reinforcing the importance of technical mastery, critical data interpretation, and delivering solutions with clarity, performance, and responsibility.

CHAPTER 25. FINAL CHECKLIST FOR THE XGBOOST PROFESSIONAL

Developing models with XGBoost requires a systematic, technical, and organized approach. At the final stages of a project, the responsible professional must ensure that all criteria for quality, stability, interpretability, and performance have been rigorously verified. This chapter provides a complete checklist, validated across multiple professional contexts, ensuring that no critical step is neglected. It is the practical consolidation of what differentiates an experiment from a model ready to generate value in production.

Essential validations must be based on the statistical robustness of the model, alignment with business problems, and operational stability. The minimum checklist includes:

- Verification of the main metric with validation data

- Comparison between training and testing performance to detect overfitting

- Evaluation with stratified cross-validation

- Testing with an external set or operational sample

- Evaluation of the model by specific classes or segments

- Calculation and review of precision, recall, F1 score, and

AUC

- Visualization of the ROC curve and confusion matrix

- Interpretation with SHAP Values, highlighting the most relevant features

- Robustness testing with injected noise and outliers

- Stability testing across repeated executions

If these validations are ignored or done superficially, the model may show good performance in testing but fail in real operational environments.

The final production stages involve a series of technical and organizational measures to enable safe and efficient use of the model:

- Saving the model with joblib, pickle, or XGBoost's save_model()

- Recording the model version, parameters, training date, and validation metrics

- Automated testing with real samples from the input system

- Validation of model input with schemas (types, formats, limits)

- Generation of a standardized prediction script for inputs and outputs

- Creation of a requirements.txt with all libraries used

- Containerization with Docker, if applicable to the deployment environment

- Clear documentation on how to use, update, and interpret the model

- Inclusion of logical fallback for inference errors in production

- Planning of a monitoring and retraining pipeline

These steps ensure that the model is not only technically valid but also operationally viable.

Before deployment, some strategic precautions should be adopted to avoid silent issues and facilitate future maintenance:

- Review production data: is the distribution compatible with training data?

- Are the operating system and libraries of the production machine compatible with those used in development?

- Are the feature names and order fixed and protected against unexpected changes?

- Was the preprocessing pipeline replicated exactly as in development?

- Is there logging of inputs, outputs, and errors?

- Is there a rollback plan in case of failure or instability?

- Do stakeholders understand the model's limits and how to interpret it?

The answers to these questions must be affirmative before moving the model into an operational environment.

Common Error Resolution

Error: Model works in Jupyter but fails when integrated into an API
Cause: Differences in environment or input format
Solution: Test with realistic JSON inputs and simulate REST calls before deployment

Error: Performance in production is worse than in validation environment
Cause: Different data distribution or undetected drift
Solution: Implement continuous metric monitoring and periodic base review

Error: Feature missing when loading saved model
Cause: Change in the order or name of columns after training
Solution: Fix feature_names and validate with automatic checking before prediction

Error: Model behaves unpredictably with extreme values
Cause: Lack of robustness to outliers or missing data
Solution: Inject adverse scenarios and reassess model stability

Error: Library update issues breaking compatibility
Cause: Environments without version control or loose dependencies
Solution: Use virtualenv, Docker, and controlled requirements files

Best Practices

- Maintain a functional copy of the model with all data and frozen scripts

- Validate the model with real data before production deployment

- Include both technical and business logs in the prediction pipeline

- Clearly document all technical decisions and parameters used

- Define a periodic reassessment plan based on operational metrics

Strategic Summary

The final checklist of the XGBoost professional consolidates a vision of technical excellence and operational responsibility. Validating, versioning, documenting, and monitoring are not optional tasks but mandatory components to ensure that the model delivers real value safely, scalably, and sustainably. By following this checklist with discipline, the professional positions themselves as a reliable bridge between data science and the generation of direct impact on systems, users, and organizational strategies. This is where technical knowledge transforms into applied competence.

FINAL CONCLUSION

Mastering XGBoost is not just about understanding its syntax or knowing how to tune hyperparameters. It is about incorporating a standard of excellence in structured data modeling, integrating performance, explainability, stability, and strategic application. XGBoost is not just a library — it is a robust foundation for models that need to deliver consistent results in demanding environments such as companies, production systems, and critical operations. In this technical manual, you have followed a structured journey to transform raw data into high-impact predictions, progressing from conceptual foundations to integration with APIs and large-scale systems.

At the beginning of the journey, the fundamentals of XGBoost, its technical motivations, boosting structure, and operational advantages over other libraries were established. The explanation of its internal workings, focusing on functional gradient descent, regularization, and parallelization, created a solid foundation for the conscious use of the tool.

The practical sequence began with data preparation. Cleaning, transformation, and encoding were treated as inseparable parts of the modeling pipeline. How each preprocessing decision directly influences model performance was presented with technical rigor and applicability.

Understanding boosting, the differences from bagging, and the specific advantages of XGBoost revealed that architecture matters — and that knowing how the algorithm builds and adjusts its trees enables confident advancement to the next phases. From installation to the first regression or classification model, operational fluidity was prioritized, allowing each reader to efficiently transition from understanding to practice.

Evaluation techniques with appropriate metrics and threshold adjustments with ROC curve analysis, AUC, and confusion matrix reinforced the book's commitment to evidence-based decision-making. Models are tools to support reasoning — and are only reliable when validated in depth.

Feature importance analysis, using gain, cover, and frequency, allowed seeing the model beyond accuracy, revealing the key elements that drive each prediction. This vision was expanded with the use of SHAP Values, transforming XGBoost into an explainable, auditable, and reliable tool for regulated environments.

Controlling overfitting with early_stopping_rounds, reg_alpha, reg_lambda, cross-validation, and automated tuning with GridSearchCV and RandomizedSearchCV consolidated model engineering as an iterative and refined process.

The technical journey advanced with multiclass modeling, integration with Pandas, NumPy, time series, and deployment frameworks like Flask, FastAPI, and Streamlit. Each chapter brought not just theory but detailed execution, with explanatory code, best practices, and structured error resolution.

GPU acceleration and distributed execution with Dask demonstrated that XGBoost goes beyond local performance. It scales with your project, whether through multiple cores, multiple machines, or cloud clusters.

Modeling in enterprise projects was addressed with responsibility: requirement gathering, versioning, documentation, team integration, and reliable deployment. The final checklist consolidated the professional behavior expected of those delivering models in real environments.

The modular structure of this manual allowed each chapter to function as an independent tool but also as part of a larger mechanism: a complete applied intelligence pipeline. The case studies, public data analyses, and operational recommendations connected theory to practice with objectivity.

As the author, I conclude this manual with a direct thank you to you, the reader. Your presence here indicates a commitment to technical excellence. May this content have served as a platform for mastery, application, and differentiation. XGBoost is a library in constant evolution — and now, with this book, you are prepared to evolve with it. May every line of your code generate impact, may every model deliver value, and may every deployment represent not only a technical delivery but an affirmation of your maturity as a data professional.

Sincerely,
Diego Rodrigues & Team!

www.ingramcontent.com/pod-product-compliance
Lightning Source LLC
LaVergne TN
LVHW022317060326
832902LV00020B/3515